THE ART OF
BUSHCRAFT

THE ART OF
BUSHCRAFT

A FIELD GUIDE TO PRESERVING TRADITIONAL SKILLS AND RECONNECTING WITH NATURE

JESPER HEDE

Translated by Kim Gardner

Skyhorse Publishing

Originally published by Turbine forlaget under the title *Bushcraft håndværk*.

Cover: Muusmann Publishing
Interior design: Katrine Bønsøe
Photos: Jesper Hede, Bushcraft Denmark
Photos leather section: Natacha Hejl
Sketches: Elizabeth Ekeklund Brondthagen and Xenia Søllingvraa

Skyhorse Publishing books may be purchased in bulk at special discounts for sales promotion, corporate gifts, fund-raising, or educational purposes. Special editions can also be created to specifications. For details, contact the Special Sales Department, Skyhorse Publishing, 307 West 36th Street, 11th Floor, New York, NY 10018 or info@skyhorsepublishing.com.

Skyhorse® and Skyhorse Publishing® are registered trademarks of Skyhorse Publishing, Inc.®, a Delaware corporation.

Visit our website at www.skyhorsepublishing.com.

10 9 8 7 6 5 4 3 2 1

Library of Congress Cataloging-in-Publication Data is available on file.

Print ISBN: 978-1-5107-7693-7
Ebook ISBN: 978-1-5107-7916-7

Printed in China

CONTENTS

FOREWORD

This book is intended for anyone with an interest in primitive outdoor life, bushcraft, and old craft skills. It is a field handbook with understandable instructions, and is intended for private individuals as well as institutions and schools as a textbook.

The book is divided into different sections that deal with projects in wood, leather, clay, and the like. You get a historical background for many of the tasks, an overview of tools and maintenance, as well as rules for access to and use of nature.

I run the company Bushcraft Danmark and have made this book in collaboration with instructors from Bushcraft Danmark, Jens Nybro, Jesper Weidick, Nicolaj Hejl, and Martin Jensen, who together have more than one hundred years of experience with primitive outdoor life, and today make a living by teaching it.

All projects in this book were made by me or in collaboration with me to provide a good firsthand explanation and understanding of bushcraft, but that is not to say that these projects cannot be done in other ways. This is precisely one of the fascinating things about bushcraft.

It takes experience and repetition to become good at many of the projects shown.

Bushcraft must be cultivated in nature.

Jesper Hede

THE HISTORY OF BUSHCRAFT

Bushcraft is a relatively new word in comparison to human history, dating back about 2 million years. From the beginning, we developed our skills, first to be able to survive, later to make life easier for ourselves. Where some skills have had little importance for human development, other skills, like being able to generate fire, have had enormous importance right up to the present day.

Humans began to migrate out of Africa, and although there is no scientific evidence, it is widely believed that this would not have been possible without being able to make fire as needed. Especially with immigration north, this was a necessity simply to keep warm.

Another very important development that came in connection with our ability to make fire as needed was the ability to disinfect water, use fire to process materials, and, not least, cook food over fire. Among other things, starch and protein are absorbed by the body much better when cooked over heat. This can be seen quite clearly in the evolution of humans around 1.9 million years ago, when we "suddenly"

got taller, our brains got bigger, and we developed skills faster, all during the period when humans are thought to have learned to control fire and cook food.

Therefore, bushcraft is not a new phenomenon, just a common term for the primitive skills that we have developed over the last 2 million years. And that's exactly what bushcraft is . . . skills.

Of course, these skills do not all originate from the Stone Age but have been developed through the Middle Ages and up to the present day. Over the past few hundred years, bushcraft has gone from being a necessary evil to being a leisure activity or hobby, again due to an important development in human history.

They talk about three green waves in outdoor life. The first occurred from about 1770 to 1840, which also coincides with the Industrial Revolution. It is quite interesting to see this connection: while many workplaces moved from the countryside to the cities, people began to open their eyes to using nature in their spare time for things like hiking, gymnastics, and picnics.

It shows that we humans crave nature and need to immerse ourselves in it and the different pursuits out there.

The second green wave took place from around 1900 to 1930, when many associations and scouting movements were created, and made a great effort for primitive craft and outdoor life. During this period, an economic and social revolution took place that was important for agriculture and crafts. Increased industrialization gave rise to an urge to maintain or return to the old crafts and nature. The latest green wave started around 1970, and has lasted until today, when, among other things, camping and hiking are popular. In the 1970s, we were hit with rising oil prices and inflation, and somewhat like we have also seen during the coronavirus crisis, people found an increasing joy in nature.

In recent years, outdoor activity, like so much else, has become wilder and wilder, and now includes adventure sports, climbing, and the like, but bushcraft has won out as the quieter part of outdoor life. This shows once again that we humans still seek nature and want to acquire skills and knowledge about it.

Today, bushcraft is a hobby for many, and a way to remove all the unnecessary things and options we surround ourselves with on a daily basis—at least for a while. Bushcraft gives us the opportunity to get back to basics and only have to deal with our basic needs: shelter, warmth, water, and food.

Being able to spend longer in nature with homemade equipment in a primitive way feels like a good experience for many. Although such a trip can be physically exhausting, you often feel mentally recharged when you get home. This has been researched, and although it can be quite difficult to put into a system, researchers have nevertheless come to the conclusion that staying in nature and creating crafts has many advantages for us.

A Norwegian study has divided this craft-making process into two categories: outdoor-based crafts and craft-based outdoor life. Outdoor-based crafts are nature experiences that focus on the use of nature in the form of finding materials and resources in nature, being able to build with them, tool handling, and collaborating with fellow hikers. Craft-based outdoor life, on the other hand, focuses on the nature experience and the joy of using equipment that you have made yourself, the joy of knowing about materials, and having experience with them, which often also results in a great respect and joy of walking in nature.

Both outdoor-based crafts and the craft-based outdoor life strengthen our ability to cooperate with others and improvise in different situations, thus improving our health, not only because of the fresh air, but also because being in nature has a calming effect.

In other words, bushcraft is good for us and for nature, if practiced correctly. The more knowledge you have about nature and the more wilderness skills you accumulate, the more you benefit from traveling in nature in a primitive way.

SUSTAINABILITY AND BUSHCRAFT

Sustainability currently gets a lot of attention, and it probably should have all along. We as humans, especially over the last few hundred years, have used the earth's resources in an unsustainable way, and we are seeing the consequences of that now. It is an important topic to illuminate in general, but also when performing bushcraft activities.

Back when humans lived in harmony with nature and were more directly dependent on it than we are today, it made much more direct sense, for example, for hunters and gatherers to only use and harvest what they needed. This made it possible for them to come back the following year and harvest the same necessities for survival. All this changed over time, especially after the Industrial Revolution, when the demand for nature's raw materials increased dramatically.

Of course, we cannot rewind time and live as hunters and gatherers again, but we should think about sustainability in our everyday lives, and to this extent, also when we cultivate bushcraft. This can be done by using nature and its resources, but simultaneously ensuring that we don't use them beyond being able to come back to the same place and do the same thing year after year.

We should also consider this with our equipment, food, and travel, and this is, fortunately, completely in line with bushcraft—a generally primitive lifestyle.

Many of the projects in this book are made with nature's materials, and I strongly encourage you to harvest materials for various projects in ways that do not damage the nature that we all love and enjoy walking in. This can be done, for example, by only using branches from large trees or thinning out small trees that already had to be removed to make room and light for other trees, by not catching more fish or shooting more animals than you can eat, by not picking all plants of a certain species in an area, and by moving without a trace.

Another advantage of bushcraft is that we form a completely different relationship with nature, maybe even a sense of ownership for it, and thus a different respect and understanding of how important it is to us and our existence, regardless of whether we are on a trip or sitting at home on the sofa.

TOOLS

In order to process nature's materials into useful things, you need to have some tools to do it with. Tools can be made in the best Stone Age fashion, but if you have five to seven different types of tools, there is actually no limit to what you can make in nature.

The most used types of tools are, of course, the knife, the ax, and the saw, but if you also have access to a Scotch eye auger and some carving tools, such as a carving knife, gouge, and adze, you quickly expand your options for making different things and instruments.

THE KNIFE

Without comparison, the knife is the most important tool we have at our disposal, apart from our brain and common sense, of course.

A good bushcraft knife is the knife you have with you when you need to use it, and there are a lot of options, models, and sizes. It is difficult to say which knife is the right one for you, it depends on the size of your hand or whether you will mainly use it for cutting, cooking, or perhaps splitting firewood. However, there are a number of design details that are good to know when choosing a knife.

As a starting point, your knife should have a continuous blade (full tang). That is, the knife blade continues down through the entire length of the knife. This makes the knife strong and ensures that the handle doesn't come loose. The blade itself should be about 4–5 inches (10–12 centimeters) long.

Something else you need to pay attention to is how the knife is sharpened. For bushcraft use, such as carving work, projects, and splitting wood, it is recommended to go for a knife with what's called Scandi grind, as shown on the next page. Scandi grind means that the blade has a wide bevel, which makes it good for working with wood and easy to sharpen.

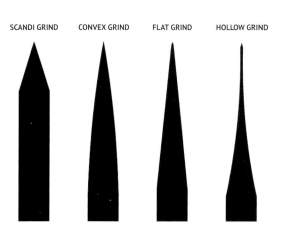

SCANDI GRIND   CONVEX GRIND   FLAT GRIND   HOLLOW GRIND

There are many different types of steel, each with their own advantages. Most people choose a knife with a carbon blade, where the steel typically contains 1–2 percent carbon. Originally, this came from the coal-fired hearth where the knife was forged, but today it is added to the steel, as it yields strong and flexible steel that is easy to get really sharp. A disadvantage of carbon steel is that it can rust. So, you should always wipe your knife after use, and occasionally apply a little cooking oil to protect it. Some of the most popular types of carbon steel are 1075, 1095, and O1.

If you use your knife a lot by the sea, it is recommended to get a knife with a more rust-resistant blade. This is most often achieved by adding chromium to the steel, and the most popular types of steel are D2, Sandvik 12C27, and K720.

THE AX

The ax is a fantastic tool that has been used since the Stone Age, when it was made from flint. Today, of course, it is made of steel and is a tool that you can fell, split, cut, and hammer with. The ax is not indispensable, but is really nice to have with you, especially when you have to build large projects. In some cases, the ax can easily be replaced by a good knife and saw.

It is difficult to give a clear answer as to what a good ax is, as it depends a lot on what it will be used for. A carving ax, which is used for all the rough work before you really start carving, must be well balanced and not too big and heavy, whereas a felling ax must be bigger and longer.

If you only want to use and carry one ax, you should go for an ax with a head that weighs 1½–2½ pounds (.7–1 kilogram) and has approximately an arm-length handle, typically 18–24 inches (45–60 centimeters) long. A good all-around ax also should not have a wedge-shaped head that is too wide, but a slimmer head, so that it can be used more easily for smaller tasks.

Axes come with both fiberglass and wooden handles. I recommend going for an ax with a wooden handle. It's not because those with fiberglass handles can't be good, but they are typically made so that you can't change them if the handle breaks. When choosing an ax with a wooden handle, you should go for a hickory or ash

handle without knots, and with a grain that runs lengthwise and not across the handle.

Just as there are ax heads for all chopping tasks, such as a broadax for hewing planks, a splitting ax for splitting firewood, a joiner's ax for carpentry work, or an adze for hollowing out, there are also different handles for these axes. Most axes have a curved handle, which means that the handle has a slight "S" shape, which provides a good grip and a good working position. The joiner's or carpenter's ax, on the other hand, often has a straight handle, which makes it more suitable for precision work.

The vast majority of axes are made of carbon steel, which is often softer and easier to sharpen, but which also rusts if you leave it in a wet state for a long time. So,

it may be a good idea to wipe your ax after use and occasionally apply a little oil. Here, you can just use ordinary cooking oil to protect it from rust.

Today, there are two major manufacturers of axes for bushcraft: Hultafors/ Hult bruks, which dates back to 1697, and Gransfors bruks, which was founded more than one hundred years ago. Both are Swedish. At flea markets and eBay, however, you can still find many exciting and good axes, like Wetterlings, DSI, and Husqvarna, that, with a little love, can be used for many years to come.

THE SAW

The saw is not a new invention, although in approximately the last two hundred years it has become a favorite tool for woodworking. Saws found from the Stone Age were made from serrated flint knives or bones and jaws from various animals. In ancient Egypt, bronze saws resembled what we call a foxtail today, dated to around 1500 BC.

Today, most saws are made of tool steel or carbon steel and come in an infinite number of variations, depending on what they will be used for. Some of the most popular in the outdoor world are folding saws and bow saws, which can be taken apart so they're easy to carry in your backpack. A good, ordinary foxtail is also fine for many tasks, but a bit troublesome to carry around.

As with the ax, you tend to buy a small folding saw like the one pictured here to avoid having too much weight in your backpack, and it is also excellent for projects and smaller tasks. A slightly longer saw, 12–20 inches (30–50 centimeters), also gives you many options for sawing larger pieces of firewood and felling trees. The longer saw doesn't add much weight and can still be used for projects.

Whether you prefer a folding saw or collapsible bow saw or buck saw is a matter of taste. However, avoid triangular bow saws, as they have a very limited sawing effect due to the frame's angle. Of course, you can also make your own saw in nature if you happen to have a blade and a little cord.

SCOTCH EYE AUGER

A Scotch eye auger is a wood drill that comes in many different dimensions. It's typically equipped with a piece of pipe at the top, in which you can put a handle or stick to turn the drill. A Scotch eye auger is a good tool that allows you to do tasks that would be difficult to perform otherwise, like fastening two pieces of wood together with a dowel or installing legs on a stool or table.

Today, the Scotch eye auger is also called a snail drill and is typically used with an electric screwdriver or drill. The drill dates back thousands of years and came in its first version as a bow drill. In other words, a spindle with an attached piece of flint or steel, a bow to make the drill rotate, and a handle to hold it all in place.

CARVING TOOLS

Carving tools come in many varieties, but what they all have in common is that they are designed in more or less the same way. A good set of carving tools contains tools to carve or chop wood, that is, remove material, both in straight cuts and curves, such as on a spoon, cup, or bowl.

A good carving knife is typically a smaller knife with a thin, sharp blade, made of carbon or laminate steel, such as Mora 120 or Mora 106. The difference between these two knives is the length of the blade. The small knife can be easier to handle for finer tasks and for less experienced people.

In addition to a good carving knife, a good set of carving tools also contains a hook knife, also called a spoon knife or hollow knife, which has a curved blade that is sharp on both or only one side. This knife is used to make indentations in wood, like in a spoon. Another good tool for this that is often less demanding to use is a gouge, like a chisel with a curve in the blade.

Before you get around to using these tools, you can use a small ax and possibly an adze, an ax with a curve, to more quickly remove material from the wood being worked on.

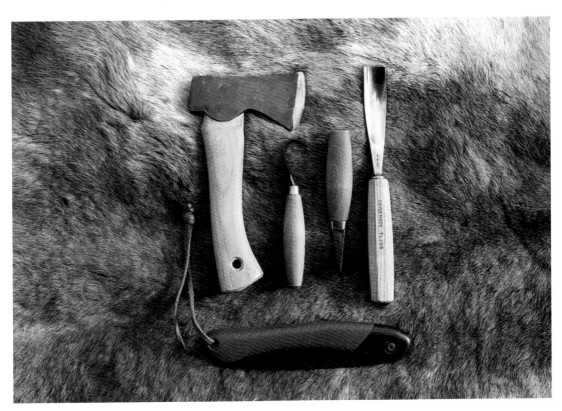

SAFE USE AND MAINTENANCE OF TOOLS

It is important to have the right equipment and especially the right tools in the wilderness, but it is equally important to be able to use them in a safe way.

SAFE USE

When working with sharp tools such as knives, axes, and saws, it is important to use them in an assured and safe manner.

THE KNIFE

The knife is the most used tool in the wilderness, so let's start with that. As children, we always learned not to cut in toward ourselves, and that's a good idea to begin with. However, it may occasionally be necessary and can be done in a safe way.

But let's start with the more common details.

An important detail, especially when sitting down and cutting, is not to cut down toward the inner thighs, as we have large blood vessels there. Instead, cut to the side of yourself and sit with your legs together.

To cut toward yourself safely, keep your elbows close to your body and cut by moving your wrists instead of your whole arm. In some cases, you can also grip the back side of the blade and press the blade through the material.

If you need to remove large pieces of material from wood, you can use a chest grip, thus using your back and chest muscles instead of your arm muscles. This is done by holding the knife and material up to your chest, then stretching your chest and back muscles in the actual cutting movement instead of just using your arms.

If you have to split smaller pieces of wood, you can also easily use a knife.

However, it requires that the blade of the knife is longer than the material you want to split.

Start by holding the knife perpendicular to the material you want to split. It is important not to hold the angle of the knife toward you, in case it slips out from under the split and hits you. Drive the knife into the material. When the blade is below the level of the material, continue to strike the outer part of the blade, while holding the knife as horizontally straight as possible with the other hand on the handle. In this way, you can split wood into very small pieces without using an ax, which can make the task more dangerous.

THE AX

The ax is the most dangerous tool we usually have with us in the wilderness, and therefore it also requires respect and consideration when using it. There are many ways to split and work with wood with the ax that are quite harmless if done correctly.

Let's start with the classic splitting technique with a chopping block. Most people have probably tried splitting firewood like this, but few have thought further about technique and safety. If you have a chopping block available, do not place the firewood in the middle of the chopping block, as the ax can slip past the chopping block, which is intended as a safety stop for the ax. Instead, place the firewood at the opposite end of the chopping block, farthest away from you. This ensures that the ax, if

it were to slip, would end up in the chopping block and not in your leg.

When swinging the ax, imagine that you're hinged at the hip and bring your entire upper body into the swing instead of just swinging the ax with your arms. This gives you a much more controlled swing and reduces the risk of hitting to the side and perhaps hitting yourself.

It can help to angle the head of the ax slightly during the swing to give the wood to be split a greater shock effect. If the wood does not split in the first attempt and the ax is stuck in the wood, it can help to turn the wood and ax so that you hit the back of the ax head down toward the chopping block, while simultaneously supporting the wood with the other hand during the blow.

If you do not have a chopping block available, you can use a fallen trunk or a thick branch as a base. Place the piece of wood you want to split on the trunk and position yourself so that you are in front of where the ax will hit the wood, so you don't hit yourself if it should slip to the side. Then, use the same technique as with the chopping block, but where the wood to be split is laying down instead of standing on the chopping block.

You can also split the wood on the long side by kneeling in front of the trunk and hitting the wood to be split where it rests on the trunk. Make sure that the wood can't tip over the trunk and hit you during the ax strike.

If you need to split smaller pieces of wood, this can be done by making a small swing with the ax on the long side of the wood at one end and bringing both wood and ax together down onto the chopping block or trunk. This is a very safe way to split smaller pieces of wood. However, make sure that you don't have your fingers between the wood and the ax handle.

If you are going to chop down a trunk, it is important to start wide. In fact, you have

to start your chop twice as wide as the diameter of the trunk to be able to chop all the way through the trunk without having to start over by hitting your own chop again.

THE SAW

The saw is the least dangerous tool we usually carry in the wilderness, but it can still cause superficial injuries, especially to the hands, and typically when you start sawing. However, this can be prevented by placing the arm you are not sawing with over the back of the blade, whether it is a bow saw or folding saw, until you have sawed below the surface of the wood with the blade. You can then place a thumb over the saw groove to prevent the blade from jumping up and possibly hitting you in the hand.

If you don't have access to a saw buck and you have a longer branch or log that you need to saw, it can help to clamp it between your thigh and calf by squatting with the log clamped firmly under your leg. Now, you can saw the log on the outside of your leg.

MAINTENANCE

Most tools are made of carbon steel, which can rust. Therefore, it's a good idea to dry the tool after use and to apply a little oil at regular intervals. Likewise, ax handles and wooden handles on knives can benefit from a little oil from time to time. Use ordinary cooking oil here, so the knife can also be used for something like cooking afterwards, without the risk of you getting sick from the applied oil. Sharp tools need to be sharpened occasionally, and there is a jungle of options, such as grinding pucks, Japanese wet grinding stones, and grinding machines, which can cost a small fortune.

There is, however, a cheap, good, and highly effective alternative that does not weigh much and makes it relatively easy to maintain knives and axes in the wilderness, namely, a piece of wet sanding paper and a leather strap with a polishing compound. For this, you need some wet sandpaper of 1000 grit or more, a piece of leather, straight stick like a slat, paint stirring stick or similar, some double-sided tape, and a polishing paste or cream such as Autosol.

Measure a piece of sandpaper and leather to fit the stick and attach the sandpaper to one side of the stick and the leather to the other with double-sided tape. Make sure it fits nicely and doesn't crease and be aware that the leather you use is not too thick and soft, as this will give an incorrect and lopsided polish. Apply polishing paste or cream to the leather side and wet the sandpaper. You are now ready to sharpen your tool.

Most knives used for bushcraft have what's called Scandi grind, a large, angled bevel on the blade that tapers straight to the edge. Other knives have what's called a flat grind or convex grind, in which the blade only has a small, thin bevel on the edge that makes the knife sharp. It is definitely easiest to sharpen the Scandi grind knife, although it may take a little longer, as you have to remove more material to sharpen the knife.

Place your sharpening stick on a firm surface and place the knife on the sandpaper. Now, angle the blade so that the bevel—the Scandi grind—lays flat on the sandpaper, then pull the entire length of the blade in a uniform movement from the sandpaper. Continue this on both sides of the blade until the desired sharpness is achieved, and finish in the same way on the leather side to polish the edge to razor sharpness. Along the way, check the edge by holding it up to the light and checking for flat spots on the edge that reflect the light. If there are flat spots on the edge, these spots require more attention and sanding.

You can sharpen your ax in the same way, but it's easier to hold the ax in your hand and guide the sharpening stick over the edge of the ax head with the other hand.

If you have to sharpen a flat or convex grind knife, it can be difficult to hit the small edge. Here, it helps to color the edge with a permanent marker, so you can always keep track of where you're sanding material away from.

In the past, you sharpened your saw yourself when it was getting dull, but with the modern and advanced sharpening of the saw's teeth and the better quality of steel, this is often an almost impossible task. It is therefore not something I recommend doing yourself.

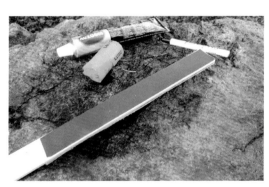

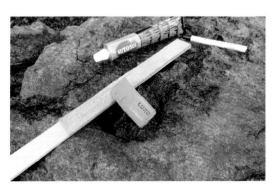

FIRST AID IN THE WILDERNESS

Knowing first aid is essential when moving in deserted areas. In fact, it is the most important survival skill, as an entirely ordinary wilderness trip can quickly turn into a real survival situation if you get hurt and don't know how to treat the injury.

In this chapter, I will review the first aid kit I always take with me on trips and have fine-tuned over the last several years. I will also review alternatives to the ordinary first aid kit and describe how to treat the most common hiking injuries, such as cuts, burns, and sprains. But first and foremost, I would recommend everyone who travels in the wilderness to take a first aid course and seek more knowledge about first aid in order to be able to save lives in the wilderness.

FIRST AID KIT

Over the years, I have traveled with many different people, some of whom do not pack first aid equipment. But you just have to realize that sooner or later you will get major or minor injuries when you use sharp tools and move in dense undergrowth or uneven terrain. Therefore, it is just as important to have equipment to deal with common injuries as it is to have your knife and fire steel with you.

Many of the things that are typically in a first aid kit can be replaced by things

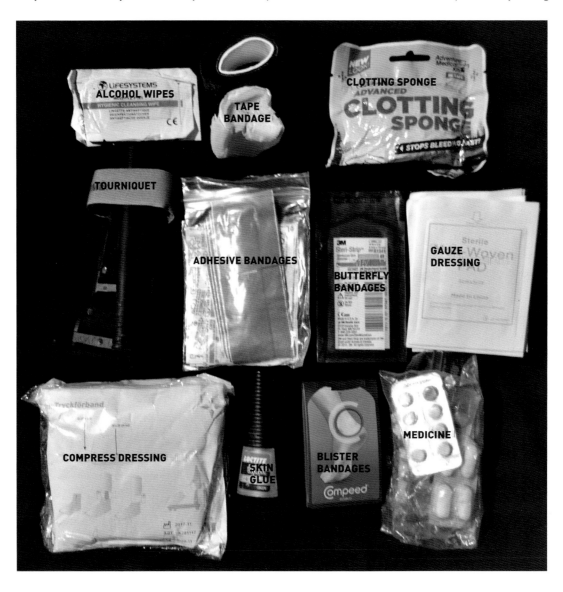

from nature or other equipment, and I will mention them here together. You should, of course, always carry a first aid kit, but on longer trips you can run out of things like bandages, and it's nice to know what else you can use.

A typical and sensible first aid kit contains:
- Wound cleaner (can be replaced with something like moss, which have a mild antiseptic effect)
- Bandages (can be replaced with moss or resin, both of which have an antiseptic effect and can effectively close small wounds)
- Compress dressing (can be replaced with moss, a bandanna, T-shirt, or similar)
- Tape (can be replaced with cord or a piece of fabric)
- Butterfly bandages or wound closures (can be replaced with tape)
- Painkillers (can be replaced with willow bark)
- Tourniquet or blood vessel clamp (can be replaced with a belt, cord, some fabric, a branch, or similar)
- Blister bandages (can be replaced with tape or regular adhesive bandage)
- Wound adhesive (can be replaced with regular skin glue, like cyanoacrylate glue, or resin).

You don't need much more in your usual first aid kit, so it doesn't weigh much or take up much space.

If you want to take your first aid kit one step further, you can add basic survival equipment like a space blanket or emergency blanket to reflect heat back to the body, a fire steel or lighter, a small water purification filter, and possibly a pocketknife.

Make sure you always have your essential gear together in one place so you can quickly take it with you if, for one reason or another, you have to leave your other gear behind. For example, if you're going out canoeing or for a hike away from the camp, all you have to do, initially at least, is think about bringing the small first aid kit with you. It will give you a much better chance of surviving in an emergency.

BLEEDING

Cuts, big or small, are probably the most common injury you can sustain on primitive tours where you use knives and axes a lot. The vast majority of injuries can be treated with a bandage, but things occasionally go wrong, and that requires a little more effort.

If you get a cut or damage a capillary (smaller blood vessel), it can usually be fixed with a bandage and maybe some tape to hold it in place. Remember to clean the wound before dressing it so it doesn't get infected.

If, on the other hand, you get a cut and damage a vein (blood vessels that carry blood back to the heart), you need to react quickly and apply compress dressing, as this kind of injury bleeds a lot.

- Press your fingers or your hand directly down on the wound.
- Lay the person down with their legs raised.
- Place compress dressing on the wound.
- Elevate the bleeding site above heart level.
- Calm the injured person.
- Protect the injured person from cold and heat loss by wrapping the person in a blanket or sleeping bag.

The same procedure applies if you get a cut and damage the arteries (blood vessels that carry blood from the heart out into the body), but the blood will pump out in spurts here, as it comes directly from the heart and therefore moves with pressure.

Injuries to arteries and veins should ideally stop bleeding fifteen minutes after the dressing has been applied.

All damage to arteries and veins must be tended to by professionals. This means the injured person must be taken out of the wilderness and to the emergency room as quickly and safely as possible.

APPLICATION OF A BUTTERFLY BANDAGE

Deeper cuts that don't bleed much can be remedied with what's called a butterfly bandage, a reinforced bandage that makes it possible to pull the wound back together. As an alternative, strong tape like duct tape can be used.

Attach the butterfly bandage to the skin on one side of the wound and pull the bandage across the wound to pull it together. Attach the bandage to the skin on the other side of the wound.

These types of wounds should also be tended to by professionals when possible.

APPLICATION OF A COMPRESSION BANDAGE

Press your fingers or your hand directly down on the wound. Lay the person down with their legs elevated and raise the bleeding site above heart level.

Apply dressing and adjust the compress to the size of the wound to get as much pressure as possible on the bleeding. Remember that the dressing must be so tight that only a little finger can fit between the gauze and the skin. If the bleeding doesn't stop, find a flat object like a stone or similar that fits the size of the wound and place it over the wound with an extra bandage or tape.

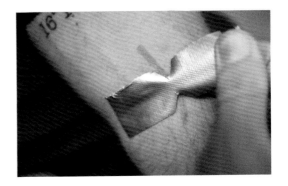

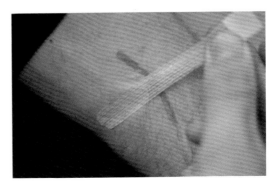

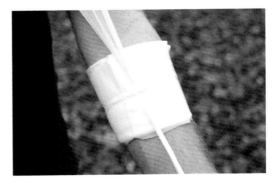

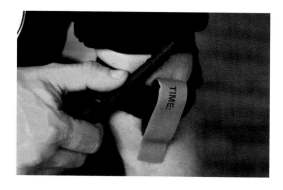

APPLICATION OF A TOURNIQUET

If the bleeding can't be stopped with a compression bandage, or if it's not possible to apply a dressing, a tourniquet (TQ) can be applied instead. The TQ should be placed 4 inches (10 centimeters) above the injured area and never on joints. If perfusion continues, another TQ can be placed closer to the heart. When the bleeding has stopped, compress dressing can then be applied.

The pressure and TQ must not be loosened and must only be used for heavy bleeding where compress dressing is not sufficient. Try to remember the time the TQ was placed and write it down on the injured person if possible. The injured person must be tended to by professionals as soon as possible.

SHOCK

If the injured person turns pale, they may be at risk of going into shock. This is a life-threatening condition where normal blood circulation can no longer be maintained. It can be caused by heavy blood loss, burns, dilated blood vessels, or reduced heart function. The symptoms of shock are fast heart rate, paleness, cold sweats, dizziness, rapid breathing, and fogginess.

Shock is treated by laying the injured person down and possibly holding the bleeding site above heart level. Make sure to maintain the injured person's body temperature, if possible, by wrapping them in a sleeping bag, emergency blanket, or something similar.

COLD

A combination of water, wind, and low temperatures can cause hypothermia. Water cools the body twenty-five times faster than air. Children, elderly people, and unconscious people are more at risk of hypothermia than others.

An internal body temperature below 95°F (35°C) is a reduced temperature, or hypothermia, and if the body's temperature falls below 89.6°F (32°C), it is a life-threatening condition.

The symptoms of hypothermia are shivering, bluish skin, reduced breathing, and reduced mobility. Try to test the injured person by pulling up the skin on the back of the hand with two fingers. Under normal circumstances, the skin should fall into place immediately after. If it doesn't, that's a sign of hypothermia.

Warm the injured person by removing any wet clothing and wrapping them in emergency blankets and regular blankets. If the person is conscious, give them something warm and sweet to drink, and never alcohol, as it dilates the blood vessels. Lie close together in a sleeping bag to warm each other up.

Frostbite is an effect of intense cold on unprotected skin, such as the face, nose, ears, hands, and feet. Unlike the effect of hypothermia where the whole body is affected, frostbite is local and can damage the skin. Frostbite is classified as either superficial or deep. Superficial frostbite affects only the skin layer. With deep frostbite, the tissue under the skin freezes into ice crystals and will die over time.

The symptoms of superficial frostbite are a pricking or tingling sensation and pain in the frozen area. Only the outermost layer of skin is damaged, and the dead skin may peel off and leave a wound.

With deep frostbite, the skin is white or waxy yellow with a grey-blue hue. The skin is cold, hard, and waxy to the touch.

Treat the injured person by gently warming the frostbitten area in blankets and clothing. Warm the frozen area with your own body heat by, for example, holding it close to your body. Never rub the spot.

40

FRACTURES AND SPRAINS

Sprains are an injury to joints, tendons, and muscles that often occur from knocks, twists, overloads, or falls. With sprains and muscle damage, there will be pain, tenderness, swelling, discoloration, and reduced mobility in and around the injured area.

Keep the injured person still, as movement can make the injury worse and make the pain worse than it already is.

Support the injured area and never try to force the joint into place if it looks abnormal, as this can damage the joint and the surrounding muscles, tendons, nerves, and blood vessels. If possible, use an arm sling in the event of a shoulder injury.

Cool with ice or a cloth with cold water. Cooling relieves pain and causes blood vessels to contract so that any bleeding is reduced. Due to the risk of frostbite, an ice pack should never be placed directly on the skin. Cool with ice or cold water for up to twenty minutes per hour, one to four times, as needed. Cooling is most effective within the first three hours.

Apply a tight compress dressing to the injured joint, but not so tight that it stops the blood supply.

If possible, elevate the injured area above heart level, as the blood supply is thereby reduced and blood doesn't drain as quickly into the damaged vessels.

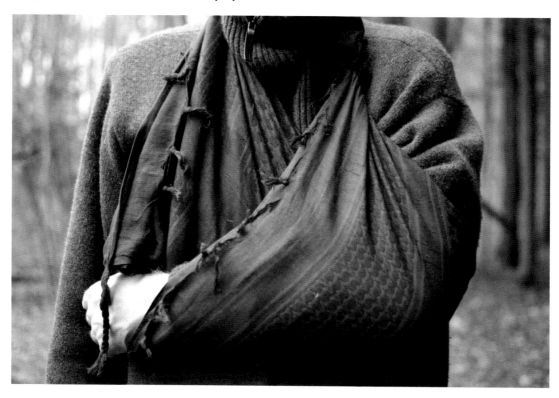

BURN INJURIES

Burns are divided into three different stages. With a first-degree burn, the skin is red and painful. With a second-degree burn, the damage is deeper and causes blisters. With a third-degree burn, all skin layers are damaged and dead. This usually requires further treatment.

In the wilderness, we most often experience first- and second-degree burns from fire. First-degree burns don't require treatment, whereas second- and third-degree burns do. They're treated in the same way.

Remove clothing from the injured area and rinse with plenty of water, preferably around 64–66°F (18–19°C). The water should be cool, but not uncomfortable. Rinse the injured area for at least one hour until it no longer hurts, but no more than four hours. If there is clothing or something else stuck in the wound, leave it there until the treatment is finished.

INSECT BITES

Insect bites are difficult to avoid when walking in nature. Mosquitoes, in particular, can be a big burden, but are rarely more than an annoyance, whereas wasp stings and tick bites are a different matter.

BEE AND WASP STINGS

Remove the stinger with a needle or by scraping with a knife; do not use tweezers. Remove tight clothing. Cool it down with an ice pack or cool compress for thirty minutes. In the event of a sting in the mouth, you can cool it with ice or cold water.

If the injured person is allergic to bee and wasp stings and has antihistamines with them, make sure the injured person takes them.

Wash the sting regularly with soap and water to avoid infection in the wound.

TICK BITES

Check your body for ticks and take a hot shower when you get home from a trip. If you have a tick, remove it as soon as possible and monitor the bite site for four weeks. If a skin rash occurs that is larger than 2 inches (5 centimeters) in diameter, or if you are in doubt as to whether you may have been infected, you should go to the doctor.

TRANSPORT

Transporting an injured person in the wilderness is almost inevitable, and if the damage is extensive, it can be a bit of a challenge.

If the injured person can leave the area themselves, make sure to relieve the person as much as possible and support the person if necessary. If the injured person cannot get out themselves, it may be necessary to carry the person out to the nearest evacuation area.

IMPROVISED STRETCHER

A stretcher can be a life-saving tool, and one that you can make with what you currently have available if a travel companion is seriously injured and is unable to transport themselves. Of course, a stretcher can also be used to transport objects such as firewood, water cans, or the like. For the type of stretcher mentioned in this book, you need two continuous logs and material to lay the person on between the logs.

The two logs or branches must be approximately 10 feet (3 meters) in length and approximately 2–2½ inches (5–6 centimeters) in diameter.

You can use different materials for the stretcher itself, depending on what you have available.

It can be two jackets that are zipped, where you insert the two logs through the sleeves and form a stretcher where the person can lie on the jackets.

You can also use two large garbage bags that you pull over the logs. Make holes for the logs in the corners of the bottom of the

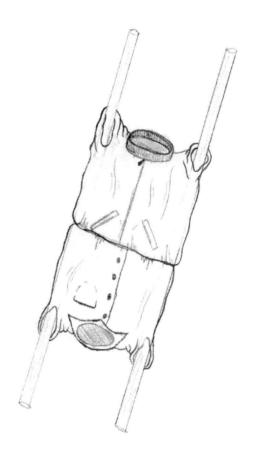

garbage bags and insert the logs that will make up the carrying handles through the holes.

Another option is to use rope or cord and tie something like paracord at a distance of approximately 24 inches (60 centimeters) between the logs in a zigzag pattern so that the person can lie down comfortably and rest on the ropes.

IMPROVISED CRUTCHES

If the injured person can walk with their injury, but not without support, it can help to find two strong, but not too heavy, Y-branches that fit under their armpits and reach down to the ground.

NATURE'S MEDICINE

It is generally a good idea to have some over-the-counter medicine in your first aid kit, like painkillers, allergy pills, and diarrhea pills. If you don't have these or have already used them up during the trip, there are plenty of alternatives in nature.

Here are the most common ones and their use.

WILLOW
Willow bark contains acetylsalicylic acid, which has a pain-relieving effect. Cut a thin branch from the willow tree and squeeze the sap out of it. It has a bitter taste but acts as a mild pain reliever. Squeeze out more sap, and possibly replace the branch once the injured person has had enough for the pain to begin to subside.

SPHAGNUM MOSS
Sphagnum moss comes in many varieties and can get quite tall. Sphagnum moss is a mild antiseptic and has been dried and used as a bandage in the two world wars. Moss often contains a lot of water and can also be used as a wet wipe due to its antiseptic effect.

BROADLEAF PLANTAIN

Broadleaf plantain has an antiseptic effect. You can use it as soap by rubbing the leaves with a little water or you can use it as a wound cleaner by chewing the leaves into a paste and applying them to an inflamed wound.

YARROW

Yarrow has a calming and fever-reducing effect and can be made into tea in the same way as wild chamomile.

CHAGA

Chaga is a fungus that grows on birch trees. It is quite rare but is also one of the most antihistamine-containing plants available. Take a small lump of the hard, woody fungus and boil it in a pot of water for ten to fifteen minutes. Drink the tea to prevent colds, allergies, and flu.

PINE NEEDLES

Pine needles contain a lot of vitamin C and work well against colds. Boil a handful of pine needles in a pot of water for five to ten minutes and drink the tea to relieve colds.

WILD CHAMOMILE

Wild chamomile has an anti-inflammatory and calming effect and is therefore suitable for treating sore throats. Take a small handful of leaves and flowers and boil them in a pot of water for ten to fifteen minutes. Drink the tea as relief from throat pain.

BIRCH POLYPORE

Birch polypore grows on birch trees and is white with a slightly yellowish or brownish surface. The underside of the fungus has a waxy or leathery surface and can be cut into suitable strips and used as a bandage on minor cuts and the like. Birch polypore is an antiseptic and can prevent and treat inflammation in a wound.

ACCESS AND RULES IN NATURE

Bushcraft is outdoor life in its simplest form and has gained more and more popularity in recent years.

We have also had much better rules regarding free tenting and access to nature in recent years, and it is quite possible to both comply with the rules and have a lot of good bushcraft experiences. It is good to know the rules before setting off with a backpack full of tools and ideas for new projects.

We all have a duty to look after nature and leave it as we would like to experience it ourselves the next time we go into the forest. "Leave No Trace" has almost become the slogan of bushcraft.

Many state forests permit you to spend the night in a tent, hammock, bivouac, and the like.

A great deal in the bushcraft world is based on and around the fire. It can be anything from cooking to keeping warm

at night and making various things like charcloth, birch tar, and resin glue. Always remember to put out the fire when you leave the area and clean up after yourself. Leave no trace.

It is, of course, assumed that you behave responsibly and cautiously toward nature, plants, and wildlife, and show consideration for other people in nature. Avoid disturbing and destroying anything. Leave no trace.

PROPERTIES AND USE OF TREES

OUTER BARK
INNER BARK WITH PHLOEM/CORK
THE GROWTH LAYER
PITH
THE AUTUMN AND SPRING WOOD

BOW
SPOON
KUKSA BOWL

It is important that you can identify trees and know their properties and uses. It can be essential to whether your project will be a success or not, because there are big differences in the properties and use of trees.

Roughly speaking, a tree consists of the crown with leaves or needles, the trunk, and the root. Trees—or woody plants, as they're actually called—differ from herbaceous plants through the woody growth of cells that occurs through the deposition of cellulose in the cell walls, among other things. Unlike herbaceous plants, trees can tolerate frost and will continue to grow year after year.

If we look at the trunk, which is interesting for several of the projects that can be made, it is structured like this.

The outer bark is the tree's outer protection and consists of dead corky cells. Just below the outer bark sits the inner bark—what's called the green bark—which is alive and contains the phloem that's used to transport liquid in the tree.

This is followed by the growth layer, where the tree grows and "puts on weight" year after year and forms annual rings. You can determine the age of the tree with reasonable certainty by counting the annual rings, as one annual ring is naturally created each year. Depending on the type of tree, it uses all or part of this growth layer to transport liquid up the tree.

After the growth layer comes the autumn and spring wood that forms the strength of the tree, and in the middle of the trunk we have the pith that consists of dead cells and often has a small diameter.

In the bushcraft community, we talk about soft and hard woods. This is a bit simplistic but works well for what we need it for. Soft types of wood are known by the fact that you can make marks in the wood with a thumbnail without much effort, which you can't do with the hard types of wood. Soft woods do not have as high a calorific value as hard woods, but they can be beneficial for things like friction fires or backpack frames and the like, where we don't want too much weight on the finished product.

Here is an overview of the most common trees and their properties.

MAPLE

Acer
Grows up to 115 feet (35 meters) tall but is often found in the forest in smaller sizes in small groups of self-sown trees and is probably most easily recognized by the five-lobed leaf on the Canadian flag.

Properties:
- Soft
- Good calorific value and good embers

Application:
- Construction projects in the camp
- Firewood

ASH

Fraxinus

Grows up to 130 feet (40 meters) and has several small leaves on the same stem. The bark is light gray or olive gray. When the tree is young, the bark is smooth, but later, it develops deep fissures and crusts. In winter, ash trees can be recognized by their black buds.

Properties:
- Hard
- Very good calorific value

Application:
- Firewood (contains very little water)
- Handles for axes and saws
- Bow building

BIRCH

Betula

Grows up to 82–100 feet (25–30 meters) tall and is easily recognizable with its white, papery bark. Birch trees grow quickly and can withstand wet regions.

Properties:
- Soft

Application:
- Birch sap and syrup
- Igniting (bark)
- Containers (bark)
- Both young leaves and inner bark are edible
- Oil (bark)
- Good for carving work
- Glue from oil in the bark

BEECH

Fagus

Grows up to 130 feet (40 meters) and has a smooth, thin, grayish bark. The beech tree is used today for everything from firewood to furniture.

Properties:
- Hard
- Very good calorific value

Application:
- Firewood
- The young leaves as well as the fruit (nuts) are edible
- Carving wood

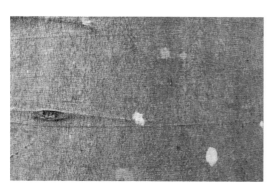

OAK

Quercus

Grows up to 115 feet (35 meters) and has grayish bark that is smooth when the tree is young. Later, the bark becomes crusty with knots and cracks. The oak tree is most easily recognized by the characteristic multi-lobed leaves and by its fruit, acorns.

Properties:
- Hard

Application:
- Firewood (good for cooking fires and embers)
- Acorns can be crushed into flour and coffee after the acid has been washed out of them
- Tanning (the bark)

ELM

Ulmus

Grows up to 100 feet (30 meters), and when the tree is young, it has a smooth, silver-grey bark that later becomes yellow-brown and rough. The leaves are oval, rough, and serrated. The tree is known in spring and summer by the fruit, samara, which is a small seed in a round, flat wing.

Properties:
- Hard

Application:
- Cord from the bark
- Samara is edible
- Bow building
- Ax handles

PINE

Pinus

Are found in many varieties and some can grow up to 130 feet (40 meters). The bark is red or orange with thin scales. Pine trees are best known for their long needles, which sit together two by two. Pine is used today mainly for building materials.

Properties:
- Soft
- Poor calorific value but burns well and quickly

Application:
- Fatwood (resinous branches)
- Tea from the needles
- The inner bark is edible

SPRUCE

Picea

There are many different types of pine trees, but spruce is one of the most widespread and important in the forest industry. Most other varieties of pine can be used in the same way. Spruce trees grow up to 130 feet (40 meters) and have brownish, scaly bark and short, green needles.

Properties:
- Soft

Application:
- Resin for glue, torch, wound cleaner, among others
- Dead, dry wood for bow drill
- Tea from the needles
- Shelter building
- Oil from small branches
- Cord from roots

HAZEL

Corylus

The hazel bush can grow up to 40 feet (12 meters) tall and is best known for its almost fan-shaped silhouette—narrow at the base and with long, straight branches that shoot up from the base. The bush can, of course, also be recognized by the nut. The straight branches are suitable for many different things and are easy to build projects with.

Properties:
- Soft
- Poor calorific value but burns quickly and hot

Application:
- Fishing rod from shoots
- Arrows from shoots
- Bow drill
- The nut is edible
- Diverse construction projects

BASSWOOD

Tilia

Basswood can grow up to 100 feet (30 meters) tall and is mostly seen in parks, but rarely in nature as a wild tree. It's recognized by the almost inverted heart-shaped crown and the serrated, heart-shaped leaves.

Properties:
- Soft
- Easy to carve with
- Poor calorific value

Application:
- Tea from the flowers
- Cord from the bark
- Tinder (kindling material) from the bark
- Good for bow drill or hand drill

WILLOW

Salix

There are approximately twenty-five willow species, and some of them appear quite different. Some are trees, while others are small or large shrubs. What they all have in common is that they often grow where it's damp—in bogs and meadows, and by lakes and streams—and have small, furry buds in the spring.

Properties:
- Soft
- Poor caloric value but burns quickly and hot

Application:
- Willow shoots to weave with
- Cord from the bark
- The bark from first-year branches acts as a painkiller
- Good for bow drill

ALDER

Alnus

Alder grows very quickly and can endure wet regions. It grows up to 82 feet (25 meters) tall and has been used for furniture, charcoal, and smokehouses, as well as bridges and pilings, due to its ability to last a long time in wet regions.

Properties:
- Soft
- Poor calorific value but burns quickly and hot

Application:
- Crafting with fresh wood
- Construction projects
- Smoking meat

FELLING A TREE

Always remember to ask permission from the owner if possible before felling even small trees. It is not always easy to fell a tree safely, at least not if it's of a certain

size. First of all, you must assess whether it's necessary to fell the desired tree. Even smaller trees can be many years old and can't simply be replaced. Do not choose a tree that is too large if you do not have experience with it beforehand. Look for a tree that is no more than 8 inches (20 centimeters) in diameter.

Start by looking at the tree and its crown, slope, and surroundings. A large crown or slope of the trunk can affect how the tree falls. Figure out where you want the tree to fall, clear the area around the tree, and make sure the tree has a free fall and won't catch on other trees.

Saw a perpendicular cut with your saw approximately halfway through the trunk

and cut a wide wedge out of the wood with your ax over the cut. This should create a weak point so that the tree will fall in the direction where the wedge is.

After this, saw an oblique cut from the opposite side with your saw slightly above the first cut and into the carved wedge. At some point, as you approach the center of the tree with the saw, it should slowly begin to fall in the same direction as the carved wedge. If necessary, help the tree a little on the way by pushing the trunk. Be ready to move away from the tree when it falls.

KNOTS

There are countless knots and hitches. However, it is not so important to know twenty different knots, nor is it so important to know how to make them, as long as they work for what you need them for. However, it can make many tasks easier to know six to seven different knots and hitches for different projects. Here are some of the most useful knots for the projects in this book and for bushcraft in general.

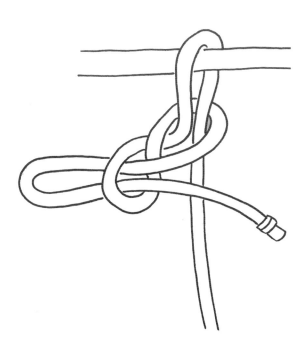

DOUBLE HALF HITCH

The double half hitch is a useful knot for something like attaching a cord to a branch or attaching an extra point on a tarp.

Start by making a loop on the cord, then make a loop a little farther on the cord and bring the last loop behind the first. Now, bring both loops down over the branch or tarp that you want to bind it to and pull both ends and tighten. You can adjust the cord and the knot by loosening it and gently pulling it in the desired direction.

 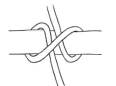 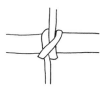

TIMBER HITCH

The timber hitch is a good knot to start many tying tasks with. The timber hitch is often used for things like pulling timber out of the forest, as it's always easy to loosen again, regardless of how much tension there has been on it.

Start by making a loop with a good length of one end of the cord. Bring the other end around that cord and twist it around itself, pulling it closed around the desired material.

As long as there's tension on the long end of the cord, the knot will hold, and as soon as there's no tension on it anymore, it's easy to loosen again.

 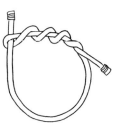 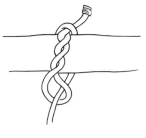

SIBERIAN HITCH

The Siberian hitch is a good knot for attaching something like a line around a tree as a ridgeline.

Start by passing the cord around the tree with approximately ½ yard of loose end. Then, hold both cords in one hand and make a loop around your fingers with the loose end. Wrap your hand around the long end of the cord and turn the back of your hand upward. Then, grab the loose end with your fingers and pull it halfway through the loop you made around your fingers. Leave a piece of the loose end hanging outside the loop and gently tighten the whole thing. Tighten the knot to the tree, and you have a Siberian hitch.

When the knot needs to be loosened, just pull on the short end of the cord, and the knot comes loose easily.

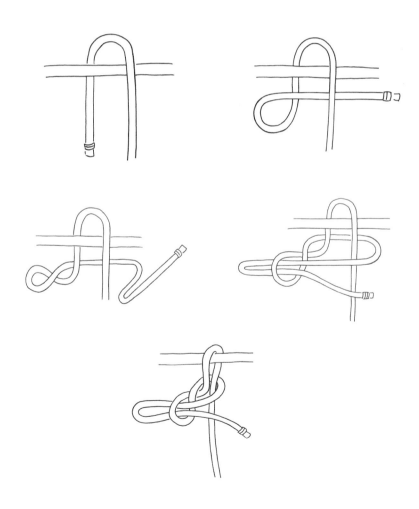

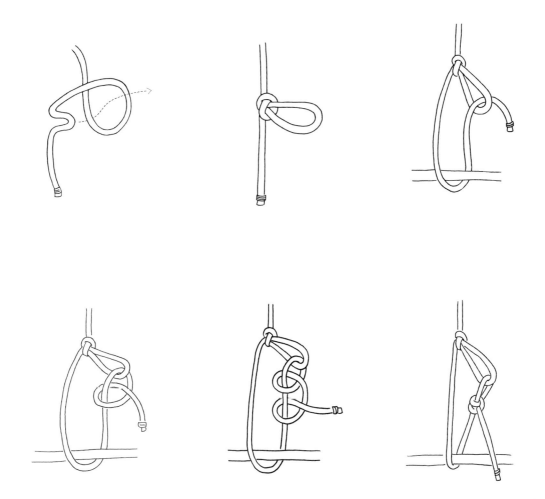

TRUCKER'S HITCH

The trucker's hitch is a good knot for something like securing loads and tightening up a ridgeline. It works a bit like a belt and is made by attaching the cord at one end with something like a Siberian hitch and at the other end with a trucker's hitch.

Make a loop on the cord approximately 12–20 inches (30–50 centimeters) in front of the tree, or whatever you want to attach the cord to. Make sure you have a long loose end, then pass it around the tree and through the loop. Now, pull the cord toward the tree and tighten the cord all the way up. Secure the cord with a slip knot or similar.

THE BOWLINE KNOT

The bowline knot is good for mooring canoes and the like. The loop in the bowline knot doesn't change size regardless of tension, and the knot is easy to loosen again.

Make a circle on the cord, leaving plenty of the loose end in excess. The length of the end determines the size of the loop. Now, bring the end from below through the loop and around the long end of the cord and down into the loop again.

A good rule to remember for this knot is that the little hare (the end of the cord) comes up from the hole, around the cord, and back down into the hole.

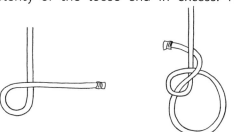  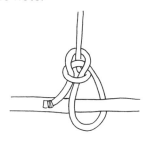

PRUSIK KNOT

A Prusik knot is a friction knot often used as a rope brake and belay when climbing. It is also good for securing a tarp on a ridgeline.

Make a loop from a piece of cord of approximately 8 inches (20 centimeters) by tying the ends together. Then, take the loop and wrap it around, say, your ridgeline at least three times, letting it go in through itself each time. Now, tighten carefully and make sure the wrap is snug. Tighten it securely by pulling on the end of the loop that is not wrapped around the ridgeline.

When there is a pull on this end, the knot should not be able to be pulled anywhere. If you want to move the knot, just take the wrapping itself and move it along the ridgeline. In this way, you can attach the corners of your tarp to a Prusik knot at each end and pull it completely tight on the ridgeline.

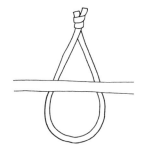   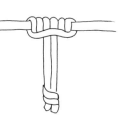

GUY-LINE KNOT

As the name suggests, the guy-line knot is usually used to adjust guy-lines on your tarp.

Start by making a small loop at one end of the cord, then pass the end of the cord through the loop and around the cord twice. Bring the end over the cord that makes up the loop and around the cord just outside the loop. Tighten it all up, and you now have the same friction effect on the cord as with a Prusik knot.

You can adjust the size of the loop by pulling the knot up and down on the cord and thereby shortening or lengthening the cord. Put a peg through the loop and into the ground and tighten it all up.

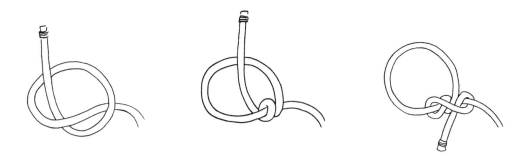

CANADIAN JAM KNOT

A Canadian jam knot works a bit like Siberian hitch and is good for tying around something like a sleeping bag or wool blanket.

Start by making a simple half hitch knot at one end of the cord. Leave a small length of extra cord after the knot. Next to this knot, make one more half hitch, and pass the long end of the cord through the new knot before tightening completely.

If you now pull on the long end of the cord, the cord should be tightened. When it needs to be loosened again, just pull the short end of the cord after the two knots.

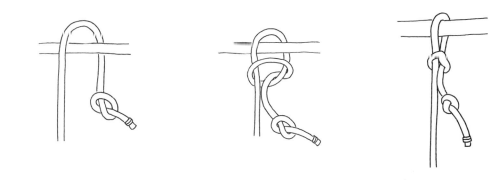

WHIPPING KNOT

A whipping knot is most often used at the end of a rope, on an ax handle, or to make an improvised handle from cord.

First, place one end of the cord in a U-shape on the material to be tied. Then, wrap the cord tightly around the material and the U-shape from the opposite end of the U-loop. When you reach the end, put the end of the cord through the U-shape and pull on the short, loose end of the U-shape at the opposite end. The excess cord can now be cut away, and you have a whipping knot.

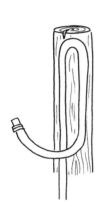 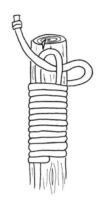 

LASHING

A lashing is used to tie two logs together, either to extend them or to intersect them. As a rule of thumb, the rope used for lashing should be as thick in eighths of an inch as the log is in inches. If the log is 3 inches (8 centimeters) thick, the rope must therefore be ⅜-inch (8 millimeters) thick. However, this is only a rule of thumb, as the required thickness also depends on the quality of the rope and what it will be used for.

A lashing must always be tied tightly so that it gives as little as possible when using the finished project.

Start by making a timber hitch on one of the two logs that has to be lashed. Now, tie the cord over the joint of the logs in a cross formation with an equal number of turns of the cord in both directions, and tie it off with something like a double half hitch.

PROJECTS

TRY STICK

Tool: Knife.

Mors Kochanski was one of the founders of what we know as bushcraft. He's behind many of the theories and projects that are taken for granted today, and throughout his long career taught thousands of people bushcraft skills. Kochanski died in 2019, but fortunately left much of his knowledge behind.

One of his projects is what's called a try stick. It's not so much a useful project when it's finished, but it's a stick on which you can practice different cutting techniques, grips, and the use of your knife.

The try stick has a total of nine different cuts that are good to know for different projects and recommended to practice. When making various cuts on the try stick, pay attention to how you handle the knife so that you don't cut yourself if it slips. Virtually all the cuts on the try stick should be made carefully and preferably with support or pressure from the thumb that is not holding the knife. See examples of different cuts in the image below.

CORD AND ROPE

Tools: Knife, saw.

Cord and rope are indispensable in the world of bushcraft. They're used for everything from building shelters to making backpack frames, bow drills, pot hangers, and nets. Over time, cord and rope have been made from many different materials, like basswood bast, hemp, wool, horsehair, and seal skin. Cord and rope made of something like basswood bast, which the Vikings preferred to use, were treated with oil from a horse's mane, and evidence has been found that this kind of cord and rope was produced and used more than ten thousand years ago.

Here are some of the most used bushcraft methods for making cord and rope.

STINGING NETTLE FIBERS

The stinging nettle stem has strong fibers on the outside of the stem that have been used to manufacture fishing line, clothing, and even bicycle tires as recently as WWII.

In order to harvest the fibers, you must first pick the stinging nettle and remove all the leaves, leaving only the stem. The stem is divided a bit like bamboo, into smaller chambers with walls between each chamber. Squeeze the stem flat so that you can open it and release the fibers. Then, break the stem in half and carefully pull off the fibers. Now, you have material to make a thin, strong cord.

PINE ROOTS

The roots of pine trees lie just below the surface of the forest floor and can be several feet long, and we can use this to our advantage by using the roots as cord.

Start by finding a large pine tree. With a branch, draw a groove in the forest floor approximately 3 feet (1 meter) from the trunk and around the tree until you meet resistance. Now, feel with your fingers whether you have grasped a root, then follow the root in both directions while you carefully dig it free from the forest floor. In this simple way, you can easily and quickly find both short and several-feet-long pieces of root that can be used for smaller binding tasks.

If the root is thick, and you want it thinner, split the root lengthwise by making a small notch at one end, then carefully pull it apart. The splitting of the root may begin to pull to one side, but this can easily be countered by pulling a little more on the strong side of the split root to pull the split back into the middle.

BASSWOOD BAST

Humans have known for more than eight thousand years to use bark for the production of cord and rope, and, especially in the Viking Age, people mainly used basswood bast for the production of rope.

Basswood bast is harvested when a tree is full of sap in June. The bast is made from the inner bark of the tree. The tree's bark consists of three layers:

- Outer bark, which is a corky layer of dead, dry cells that protects the tree from drying out and from injury
- Cork growth layer, which divides the cells of the bark and forms dead, air-filled cork cells on the outside and living, green bark cells on the inside
- Inner bark or bast, which consists of living cells that transport the sugars that are formed in the leaves down to the places where they are to be used for growth in the trunk, branches, roots, and fruit.

When you have cut the bark off the trunk or branches of the basswood tree, it must be soaked in lukewarm water, 65–68°F (18–20°C), for approximately three weeks to dissolve the binder that holds the cork and bast layers together. After three weeks, the basswood bast can be pulled off the outer bark easily, rinsed thoroughly, and dried. When the bast is dry, the individual bast layers can be separated with the fingers. The bast is now ready for use and can be used in the same way as stinging nettle fibers (page 76).

GRASS

If you need to make a quick and slightly thicker rope, it can easily be made from long grass, which is usually easy to harvest, especially in late summer and autumn. Use the same technique as with cord made from something like nettle fibers, but with a bundle of grass.

TWO-PLY CORD

Plying cord from something like stinging nettle fibers, willow bark, or pine roots is a simple but time-consuming process, but being able to produce cord in nature is a good skill to have. Regardless of the type of material you want to use or have access to, the procedure is the same.

Start by preparing the material you want to make the cord from, in this case, stinging nettle fibers. Clean the stem of impurities and try to find pieces that don't vary too much in thickness.

Now, start plying and twisting the stem in opposite directions with your thumbs and forefingers. Don't start in the middle, as you don't want to have equal length ends on the cord if you have to lengthen the cord down the road.

Ply and twist the material until it kinks or twists around itself. Now, hold the cord with your thumb and forefinger where the two parts of the cord cross each other, and twist one of the cords around itself, away from you.

Now, place this cord over the other, then twist it in the same way. Keep doing this and you will soon see the two pieces wrap around each other and start to resemble cord as we know it.

When one of the ends is about to run out, insert a piece of new material (a new stem) with a ¾–1¼ inches (2–3 centimeter) overlap on the old material, and continue to ply and twist the cord.

The reason the ends shouldn't be the same length is because gathering it in the same place would form a weak point on the cord.

This way, you can easily and simply, and without tools, make cord for things like building shelters, a tripod, or something similar.

THREE-PLY CORD

Three-ply cord is typically used in regular rope and is a bit more involved to make than two-ply cord. This technique is most often used to make cord for rope or to make thinner rope thicker and stronger.

Here, you have to use a tool, a "rope spinner," which is basically just two branches put together. Find two branches with a length of 8–12 inches (20–30 centimeters) and a diameter of about ¾–1¼ inches (2–3 centimeters). Now, split one of the branches all the way down the middle with a knife. Then, cut an indentation on each of the split sides, approximately 2 inches (5 centimeters) down from the top of the branch. On the second branch, opposite to the first, cut an indentation approximately 1¼–1½ inches (3–4 centimeters) down the branch, so that the cut piece fits into the indentations made in the split branches, so that it can rotate without too much resistance. Tie the split branch back together. Now, cut a small notch about 2 inches (5 centimeters) from the handle of the rope spinner that can hold the cord in place when it needs to be plied. Find a branch on a tree or pound a long stick into the ground and hammer a small nail into the stick that can hold the cord at the opposite end of the rope spinner when the rope needs to be plied.

Measure the desired piece of cord to be wound into a rope and tie it together at the end. Be aware that the finished rope should only be about a third of the length of the connected cord that you started with.

Now, mount one end of the cord on the branch with the nail, and the other end on the rope spinner, and start plying the rope. Also, pay attention to the direction in which the rope is plied. As you ply the rope, pay attention to when the rope starts to tighten. You can see this by looking at how far up the cords on the rope are twisted, or by loosening the rope a little and seeing if it kinks or twists around itself. When it starts to do this, go approximately a third down the rope and lay it over the rope spinner so

that you have three thinner cords from the rope spinner to the branch with the nail.

Ply the rope again, but the opposite way this time, and you should now see the rope begin to form into its final shape. Finally, tie the ends with a piece of string to prevent them from unraveling again, and you now should have a strong three-ply rope with many uses.

TRIPOD

Tools: Saw, possibly knife.

A tripod, in all its simplicity, is three branches or logs that are attached to each other at one end. It can be a useful tool for many things, like a fire stand, teepee, game suspension, and much more.

It can be made in several ways, either by tying the three logs together with cord or a fresh, flexible branch, or by finding three Y branches and locking the Ys together at the top.

If you choose to tie them together with cord, which is undoubtedly the strongest solution, you can tie them together with a figure-eight lashing, which can be made the following way: start by placing the three logs next to each other and raise one end slightly above the ground so that you can work with the cord more easily. Then, make a timber hitch around one log and run the cord alternately over and under the logs at least three times.

The cord should then run around itself between the logs and tighten up. Here, it can help to use a stick around which the cord is wrapped, to provide a better grip and tighten the end more firmly. The whole thing ends with a double half hitch.

If you choose to tie the tripod with a fresh branch or pine root instead, it is easiest to tie the tripod while it's standing up, and here you may have to improvise a bit until you have a stable tripod. The same applies when you use Y branches for the tripod and thus don't tie it. Here, the three Y branches must be intertwined to become stable.

FIRE HOOKS AND STANDS

Tools: Saw, knife.

Fire hooks come in many varieties and can make life a little easier when cooking over a fire. Here are three simple fire hooks you can make in nature.

POT HOIST

Start by cutting a piece of cord the same length as your tripod for the fire. Tie a bowline knot at one end of the cord so it can hang on the tripod. Also tie a bowline knot at the other end and find a small stick approximately ¼–¾ inches (1–2 centimeters) in diameter and 2 inches (5 centimeters) in length.

Take your pot and pull the cord through the handle of the pot. Now, bring the end with the bowline knot up on the cord over the pot handle, and insert the cord through the bowline knot so that it forms a small eye. Then, put the stick through the eye to lock the cord. Now, your pot should hang on the cord above the fire, and you can adjust it up and down by holding the knot in the bowline knot and running it up or down.

FIRE HOOKS

Fire hooks make it easy to take the pot off and on the tripod. They can be made like this: find two sticks with small side branches and cut them off as shown in the picture. Turn them any way necessary to form a hook, put them up against each

FIRE STANDS

Fire stands are intended to make it easier to use and handle kettles, pots, and pans over the fire. They come in many different kinds and with slightly different properties.

One of the very classic ones is the one with two Y branches that are fixed in the ground and have a straight overhead branch that rests in the two Y branches. It is simple to make and can be upgraded by using another Y branch as an overhang, which at one end locks the two Ys together. In this way, you can do something like tie a roast to the branch and just turn it ⅓ at a time by rotating the overlying Y branch to cook the roast evenly on all sides. At the opposite end, you can also put a pot with a handle on the branch and make side dishes for the roast.

If you want an adjustable fire stand, there are several good options for these, such as the aforementioned fire hook mounted on a tripod. You can also make a stand from a single branch that stands over the fire, angled upward, either fixed in the ground with stones or lying in a Y branch with some weight on the end that stands on the ground.

The tip of the branch that should be centered over the fire should have a flat cut so it can be parallel to the ground. You should also use a longer branch with a side branch to form the fire hook that will be at the end of the cut branch. Use your knife to score some crosses in the branch, approximately ¼ inch (5 millimeters) into the wood and carve away three triangles of the material until a row of hooks appears on the branch, just like when you carve a peg.

other, and cut the parts that will sit against each other flat.

Now, make a tight lashing around the sticks so that they're firmly attached to each other. You should now have a fire hook that can be hung from the cord on the tripod and placed on the handle of the pot.

If you have no more cord available, the two branches can also be taped together. This can be done by first making two small oblique cuts in one stick and carving out the material between the cuts. Here, it is important to measure precisely that one stick fits perfectly in the opposite stick, a bit like a puzzle. Now, put the two sticks together carefully and you should have a fire hook without the use of cord.

One of these hooks can be hung on the cut surface of the branch that stands over the fire. You can adjust the fire hook up and down by choosing the hook that fits the height in relation to how close to the fire the pot should hang.

Here are some more pictures of different fire stands for inspiration.

SHAVING HORSE

Tools: Ax, saw, knife, Scotch eye auger.

A shaving horse is a practical tool for hold-ing items, in this case cut wood, so that you can work on a project with both hands. The origin of the shaving horse is quite uncer-tain, but it was depicted and described for the first time in Germany in 1485 and has since been used by various craftsmen for processing things like wood and copper.

The shaving horse is a fantastic tool when you need to make something like a bow or large spoon. Today, there are many designs for shaving horses in different sizes and materials, but if you want to make one in nature from raw materials, this design is the easiest to go for.

Start by finding a trunk from a tree of a diameter and length that, when split, pro-vides a comfortable place to sit and work. Typically, a trunk with a diameter of about 12–16 inches (30–40 centimeters) and a length of approximately 5 feet (150 centi-meters) would be appropriate.

Next, split the trunk in half. Start with the ax, and when the trunk slowly begins to split, it can be helped on its way with a number of wooden wedges that you drive in as the trunk splits farther and farther down.

When the trunk is split, make some legs for it. You can make do with three

legs, two at the back and one at the front of the shaving horse. They should be made of logs or solid branches in a length that fits with a good sitting height. The legs can be mounted in the trunk by drilling three angled 1-inch (25-millimeter) holes with your Scotch eye auger to provide a wide, stable foundation for the shaving horse.

The logs for the legs should be carved on one end so that they're cone shaped and fit the holes in the trunk. The cone-shaped logs can be tapped into the trunk, and due to the cone shape, they will be held by friction. Now, you have a three-legged bench and can straighten the top and work area of the bench with your wood knife so it's nice and even.

The next step is to begin the actual device that holds the work piece. Use a strong branch of 2–2¾ inches (5–7 centimeters) in diameter that can be split lengthwise to form the two arms of what is probably most easily explained as a ladder with three steps. The middle step is attached to the shaving horse, and the upper step is used to hold the work piece by stepping on the lower step. More on that, later.

Now, you can use your wood knife to straighten the two split branches so that they're nice and even. Then, with the Scotch eye auger, drill three holes in the two split branches, one at each end, approximately 2 inches (5 centimeters) from the end of the branch, and one in the middle. Make sure to measure so that the ladder can be mounted on the shaving horse with smaller branches through the middle hole and into the shaving horse and can swing freely on the bench without touching the ground. Once this is done, drill a hole on each side at the desired location on the shaving horse (perhaps try sitting on the shaving horse and get a feel for where it would be appropriate to have the hinge for the ladder).

Once these holes have been drilled, cut two branches that can be friction-locked into the holes. These branches will form the hinge for the ladder. In addition, you need a branch cut to size for the top of the ladder, and a longer one for the bottom of the ladder. The longer one will form the

footrest that, by pressure, holds the material you want to work on firmly under the top branch of the ladder.

Now, it's time for the trickiest part of this project: getting it assembled all at once. Install the lower step first, as it is the longest, then install the two large branches with the holes on them that make up the hinge at the same time you install the upper branch. This may take some time, and the final result should preferably be such that it all sits securely together and reasonably close to the body of the shaving horse.

Finally, a plank must be mounted on which the object you will later work with can lie in tension under the upper part of the ladder. Such a plank can be split from a piece of trunk, a strong branch, or a strong board. The plank can be attached to the front of the shaving horse, approximately 2 inches (5 centimeters) from the edge, by drilling a hole with the Scotch eye auger through the plank and down into the trunk, then securing it with a branch cut to size. The angle of the plank is important to get a good working position and must be supported by a wooden wedge or similar that can then be adjusted back and forth.

You should now have a finished shaving horse that you can enjoy for many years. The shaving horse is used in such a way that the item you want to work on can be secured between the plank and the top step of the ladder. When you then step forward on the bottom step of the ladder, the work piece is held firmly, and you can work with something like a wood knife or gouge on the work piece.

HOLD DOWN

Tools: Knife, saw, Scotch eye auger.

A hold down is exactly what the name suggests, a device to hold a work piece firmly on its chopping block. Usually, it's made from a curved piece of steel, but it can also be made easily in nature from a solid branch with a side branch adapted to function in the same way as steel. This little wooden device was invented by my instructor and good friend, Jesper Weidick.

Start by finding a solid branch with a corresponding side branch. The branch must have a diameter that is slightly larger than your Scotch eye auger. Now, drill a hole with your Scotch eye auger in your chopping block, and cut the main branch so that it becomes slightly cone-shaped and fits into the hole on the chopping block.

Saw off the side branch to a length so that it can form the securing part of your hold down. Put the main branch down on the hole to measure where it makes sense

to saw off the side branch. Be sure to make a flat and even saw path here so that the top of the branch can get as much contact with the work piece you wish to hold down.

You can attach material under the side branch by putting the main branch down into the hole on the chopping block. This can help if you want to do something like use a wood knife to make spoons or want to have both hands free to work with your gouge on something like a kuksa.

SWEDISH LAP VISE

Tools: Scotch eye auger, cord, wooden board or a split piece of wood.

A Swedish lap vise can probably be explained most easily as a simplified and transportable shaving horse. It is, in all its simplicity, a wooden board with some holes, 2 inches (5 centimeters) apart, in the center of the board. The board could also be made by splitting a slice from a log. Fit a cord through the holes and tie together into a loop of a suitable size so you can place the board on your lap when you sit, attach an object between the holes and under the cord, and step into the loop and press down with your feet to secure the object.

You can now use both hands to work with things like a wood knife. At the same time, you're protected by the board and aren't easily injured if the knife were to slip.

If you want to raise your work piece a little, make a wooden wedge and insert it under the work piece that's under the rope and clamp both parts firmly by stepping into the loop.

SIMPLE SAW BUCK

Tools: Ax, saw, knife.

Having a good place to stand when sawing firewood or doing something like debarking logs makes the task much easier and it can be done with a simple saw buck.

Start by finding two good logs approximately 5 feet (1½ meters) long, and chop the ends so that they can be tied together in an inverted V. Now, tie two smaller logs or branches across the top of this inverted V, as shown in the picture. The distance between the logs should be slightly larger than the object you later want to work with.

This inverted V can hold your work piece steady if you feed it between the two cross logs and let the work piece and saw buck act as a tripod. You can now saw, debark, or cut the work piece at a good working height, and continuously adjust the height of the work piece by changing the angle of the saw buck.

SPOON

Tools: Saw, ax, carving knife, gouge or spoon knife.

Carving a spoon in nature has almost become the mascot of bushcraft and is also an enjoyable process, especially in the dark hours around the fire, when it can be difficult to do many other projects. Over time, many—including yours truly—with more or less success, have tried to carve a spoon without fully knowing the process involved. Here's how to do it so you don't have to make the same beginner mistakes as so many others.

In theory, you can carve most types of wood, but there are some that are much better than others, such as birch, which is a relatively soft and flexible wood. Other types of wood, such as cherry, beech, and oak, are somewhat harder to carve, but can also produce great results with an exciting play of color and grain.

As a starting point, you should avoid using the heart of the tree for carving projects, as you run the risk of the wood splitting and losing strength when it dries. Fresh wood is easier to carve than dry wood.

The right tool is, as they say, half the job. Many people start with their usual knife and perhaps a spoon knife, but with a small investment in a real carving knife such as a Mora 120 or Mora 106 and a gouge (a chisel with a curved blade) you will go a long way. A small ax also makes the task much easier.

Start by finding a piece of fresh wood without knots and branches. Split it out so that you end up with a square piece of wood that doesn't contain heartwood.

Most spoons are slightly curved—or S shaped, if you will—when viewed from the side. Now, draw the desired curve on the side of the cut wood and saw the desired

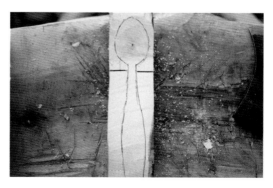

depth where the bowl of the spoon should be. Now, use the ax to chop the excess material away until you get your desired curve.

Draw your desired spoon pattern on the other side of the wooden block and saw two stop cuts behind the bowl of the spoon. Stop sawing $\frac{1}{16}$–$\frac{1}{8}$ inch (1–2 millimeters) before the drawing ends.

Then, use the ax to remove most of the excess material. Leave $\frac{1}{16}$–$\frac{1}{8}$ inch (1–2 millimeters) here, as well, so you don't run the risk of chopping into the wood that will end up being the spoon.

It is important, both when using an ax and a knife, to carve in the right direction in relation to the grain of the wood, as shown here.

Now, the spoon is ready for the carving work itself. Carve the spoon to the desired shape and remember to keep paying attention to the direction of the carving in relation to the grain and fibers of the wood.

When the shape of the spoon has been carved, it's time to carve the indentation itself in the spoon. Here, it's important to carve across the grain of wood as far as possible and not to make the indentation so deep that the spoon becomes uncomfortable to eat with. If you wish, take the first few times to use an ordinary spoon as a template, and look at the depth and shapes. For the indentation in the spoon, both a gouge and a spoon knife or hook knife can be used, or a combination of both. Expect it to take a few tries and a bit of practice to get a really nice result.

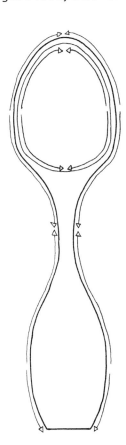

Carving directions

KUKSA

Tools: Ax, saw, carving knife, gouge, possibly adze.

The kuksa is a cup carved from a tree burl, typically from birch. The tree burl is really just a misshapen branch that forms criss-cross wood fibers, as opposed to an ordinary branch that has relatively straight fibers. This also means that it becomes stronger and has less risk of splitting during the drying process. It can also be made from ordinary wood, as shown here.

Start by finding the piece of wood you want to make the kuksa from. Choose a piece of wood without a lot of knobs and side branches, as they can give you a leaky or cracked cup later. Split the wood in half so you avoid using the pith (the middle of the trunk) and chop the top flat so you have a good starting point to work from. Then, draw the shape and size of the kuksa on your piece of wood, and start shaping the kuksa with the ax. Feel free to take the trouble to draw the kuksa both from the top and bottom and, later in the process, also from the side.

When using an ax and knife, be careful to always chop from the highest point, and down toward the lowest point, so you don't chop into the veins, as you risk splitting off more wood than you want. Use the ax as much as you feel you can and always think about where you place your thumb, as it's usually the one finger most prone to a wrong chop or cut.

When the basic shape of the kuksa is chopped out, start hollowing out the cup itself with an adze (an ax shaped like a large gouge that can help with the coarser excavation work), then switch to a gouge and possibly a hook knife or spoon knife. Be aware that these tools work best across the grain of the wood and not along the kuksa.

Once you have hollowed out a bowl in the kuksa that suits your desired purpose, start removing material and start the first finish on the outside of the kuksa. The thickness of the wall of the cup can vary greatly and is somewhat a matter of taste. Remember to carve from the highest to the lowest point here, too, so that your wood doesn't start fraying.

When you feel the kuksa is done, leave it to dry. The drying process must not go too fast, as you risk the cup splitting. Place the kuksa in an open bag, possibly with some of the fresh shavings, and store it in a not-too-hot and not-too-ventilated place. Now, it's about having patience. Let the kuksa dry over a few weeks until it feels completely dry, warm, and light.

If you don't finish the project all at once, you can store the kuksa in the fridge or even the freezer, which stops or drastically delays the drying process, so you can continue working on it later.

When the kuksa is dry, you can make the final finish on it and possibly sand it with sandpaper on the inside. The dry wood is harder to carve, but at the same time also gives a nicer finish.

It's a good idea to test the kuksa before you use it. If it's not completely dry and you pour boiling liquid into it, the moisture in the wood could expand and you risk it splitting. Some swear by putting it in a pot of water and slowly heating it up to the boiling point. Others dry it completely at low temperatures in the oven at the end of the process, while others cross their fingers and grab a cup of hot coffee.

Finish the kuksa with oil to help prevent it from being discolored so easily by the liquids poured into it. Be careful not to use olive oil, as it will become rancid and gummy over time. I recommend using walnut or almond oil instead.

PLATE

Tools: Ax, saw, carving knife, gouge.

A plate is a nice piece of equipment to take on a trip to prepare and eat from, and it doesn't get much better than if you carve your own. This way, you get the size, design, and depth you want.

Start by finding a suitable piece of wood. It can be a trunk from a birch, cherry, ash, or similar tree. Split the trunk in half, then split one half out farther so that you get a flat board to work with. Avoid using the pith (middle of the trunk).

When splitting a piece of wood, it's important that there's equal mass on both sides of

the split to give an even split through the grain of the wood. If there is less mass on one of the sides, the wood tends to split on the side with the least mass. It may therefore be necessary to split the trunk more times to achieve your desired thickness.

Once you have a board of your desired thickness, trace the shape of the plate onto the board and begin removing excess material with the ax. Remember to always cut from the highest point to the lowest point, so you don't cut along the veins or fibers of the wood, as you otherwise risk the wood splitting where you don't want it to.

Once you've made a rough shape of your plate with the ax, you can start making the desired indentation in the plate. This is done most easily with a gouge across the grain of the wood. If you use the gouge with the grain, you will find that the wood frays and makes the process slower and more difficult.

Continue with the design and the initial finish on the outside. The plate must then be dried. This is best done in an open bag, possibly with some fresh shavings in it. Let the plate dry slowly and store it in a place that is not too hot and not too ventilated.

Finish the plate with oil to help prevent it from being discolored so easily over time. Be careful not to use olive oil, as it will become rancid and gummy over time. I recommend using walnut or almond oil instead.

HANDLE FOR CARVING KNIFE

Tools: Auger, knife, saw, ax.

A handle to a knife blade is not at all as difficult as one might think and can be done easily in nature. However, this method requires an auger and, of course, a knife.

You need a fresh piece of wood, in this case, a piece of birch. Start by sawing out a piece that is slightly longer than the tang on the knife blade. Now, measure the length of the tang and mark the auger with tape so that you don't drill too deeply. Be very careful here to drill as straight into the wood as possible. Then, split the piece out

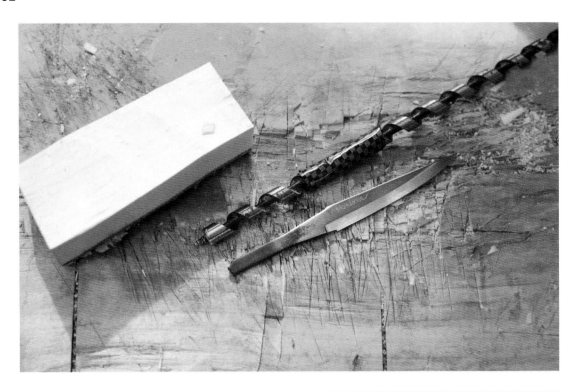

to a suitable size so that you don't have to carve so much to adjust the handle later.

Gently tap the handle on the blade and cut two small dowel pins from dry wood to hold the blade in place. Possibly carve away excess material from the pins. Use something like a stick to tap the pins down.

Now, wrap the blade in tape and carve your handle to the desired shape. As the fresh wood begins to dry, it should contract around the tang of the blade and hold it in place without the use of glue.

BACKPACK FRAMES

Tools: Saw, knife, possibly ax.

In the past, there were no modern ergo-nomic carrying systems as we know them today, but it was soon discovered that it was an advantage to have a frame on the back when heavier objects such as equip-ment, game, and water had to be carried over longer distances. Therefore, there are also many different models of primitive backpack frames.

In this section, some of the most used and well-known backpack frames are shown, as well as a few not-so-well-known ones.

THE ROYCRAFT FRAME

Probably the best-known backpack frame is named after Tom Roycraft, who invented this simple but surprisingly comfortable frame to walk with. Tom Roycraft was an instruc-tor in the Canadian Armed Forces and good friends with Mors Kochanski, another of the founders of modern bushcraft.

The Roycraft frame consists of three branches, two of them an arm's length, from fingertip to armpit. The last branch should be slightly wider than your hips. Lay the three branches on the ground so that they form a triangle, overlapping each other by a few inches. Mark with your knife where they overlap and saw two small notches on either side of the branches, carving away the material between the notches so the branches fit snugly together. Then, tie the branches together with a cross lashing.

Now, you have your backpack frame and just need a carrying system, which can be made in several different ways. If you have a piece of rope available, it can be used

105

easily by finding the center of the rope. In the style of a Prusik knot, fasten the center of the rope at the top of the backpack frame. Now, you can take the frame on your back and pass the two loose ends of the rope around the lower part of the frame and tie the ends at the front of your waist to form a kind of hip belt.

BACKPACK FRAME

This frame is like the frames we know from today and works very well. You need two straight branches with a diameter of approximately ¾–1¼ inches (2–3 centimeters) and of approximately an arm's length. In addition, you must use three branches of the same thickness, but of approximately a forearm's length.

Take one of the short branches and mark it at both ends where it goes beyond your hip width. Then, mark the other two short branches in the same length and saw two grooves ¾–1¼ inches (2–3 centimeters) apart, approximately ⅜-inch (5 millimeters) deep. Now, carve away the material between the cuts and lay the branches on the ground.

Measure the long branches to an arm's length and place them on top of the short branches to form the sides of your backpack frame. Mark the long branches where they cross the short branches and make corresponding cuts in them. Now, tie the frame together using cross lashing.

Once the frame is tied together, you need a support system for it. This can be done with a pair of trousers, a pair of socks

tied together, or with a rope, as shown here. Mount the rope on the very top of the short branches on the frame. Now, pull the rope over both shoulders and pull it down around the joints at the bottom of the frame, tying it together at the front with a bow knot. You now have a good frame on which you can mount something like your pack or other heavy equipment.

SIBERIAN PACK FRAME
Tools: Knife, possibly saw.

The Siberian pack frame is a super simple backpack frame that's made from a branch or small tree, and can be used for transporting meat, game, or firewood back to camp.

Start by finding a flexible branch or a small tree with a diameter of ¾–1¼ inches (2–4 centimeters) at the base. Then, bend the branch in a large U so it will fit on your back. Next, bend the wood fibers, so the thick part of the branch can form the base of the backpack frame and tie it securely together. Here, pine roots could be used.

Now, you need a slightly stronger branch of 8–10 inches (20–25 centimeters), possibly the excess material from the backpack frame. The support system itself, such as a rope, should be attached to this branch.

The branch can now be inserted under the arc in the backpack frame, and the rope can now be tied around the bottom of the backpack frame and form shoulder straps and possibly a hip belt.

YUKON PACK

Tools: Possibly knife.

A Yukon pack is a pack or backpack made of something like your tarp, with your equipment inside. It's tied together with cord and has a simple carrying system. The Yukon pack is also called The Hudson Bay Company pack and originates precisely from that time in the 1800s, when, among other things, The Hudson Bay Company used it to transport fur and equipment.

The Yukon pack is a simple backpack made from some of the equipment that you carry with you anyway and use for other things. You will need a tarp or a wool blanket, some cord along with a piece of rope, and a pair of socks or pants that can be used as a carrying system.

Lay the tarp out on the ground. Gather your gear in the middle of the tarp and think about how to pack it so it's comfortable to carry on your back later. After this, fold what will be the bottom of the Yukon pack on the tarp over the equipment. Then, fold the sides of the tarp tightly around the equipment, and, finally, fold the top of the tarp down over the equipment to end up with a waterproof package.

Now, tie it all together with cord across and lengthwise, and make sure to tighten it all up. Pay extra attention that the bottom of the tarp is firmly attached and doesn't

fall out when you start walking with it. There are several different ways to tie the tarp together. One method is to make large double half hitches around the package and pass the cord farther down and up around the bottom and top of the package.

Now, a support system must be installed, and this can be done in several ways. If you have a 6–10-foot (2–3-meter) piece of rope, you can run it lengthwise around the entire pack, preferably on the inside of the tied cord to secure it better, and gather it at the top and use the ends as shoulder straps, as shown here.

Then, pass the ends of the rope around the cord at the bottom of the backpack, and tie the ends of the rope on your hip like a hip belt.

If you don't have rope available, you can use a pair of socks with a few stones at the bottom. Tie them together at the top and mount them to the top of the backpack with a few pieces of cord to extend them down to the bottom of the backpack. The same applies with a pair of pants—here, the legs of the pants can form the shoulder straps and be attached to both ends of the backpack.

Be aware that it is not so easy to get to your things without having to take the whole backpack apart, so it can help to have a drinking bottle, knife, and other things hanging on the outside of this pack.

BACKPACK BASKET

Tools: Saw, knife.

A backpack basket, also called a pack basket, is a typical woven basket that you carry on your back like a backpack and can keep your equipment in. Over time, it has been made and used in many places around the world—in most places in pretty much the same design, but, of course, from available materials such as ash, bamboo, willow, and the like.

You can make a backpack basket from hazel or willow relatively easily and quickly. The frame for this basket is made of branches, between which cord and strips of leather or rawhide are woven. You will need six branches of hazel or willow with a diameter of approximately ⅜ inch (1 centimeter) and a length of 4–6 feet (1½–2 meters). The branches are best in spring, when they contain more liquid and are more flexible. If they're harvested at another time of the year, test their flexibility by gently bending them and letting them soak in water for ten days to regain their flexibility.

Start by debarking the branches, since the bark will fall off when they dry anyway. This can be done with the back of your knife or folding saw. Now, continue to bend three circles of the three thinnest branches you have. Do it carefully and support them with your hands and your body during the process so they don't break. The diameter of these circles will make up the diameter of your finished basket, and one of the three circles should be slightly smaller than the others, as it will form part of the bottom of

the basket. Now, tie each of these branches together in the desired shape and leave them for a few hours so they hold their shape better.

The other three branches can now be bent into a U shape and stuck in the ground at a width that approximately corresponds to the diameter of the circles. Now, tie each of the branches so they hold the desired U shape. Take them out of the ground and let

them lie for a while so that they keep their shape better. After a few hours, you can start to work with the branches. Start by tying the three U-shaped branches together at a cross in what will become the bottom of the basket. Then, adjust the circles inside the basket at regular intervals from bottom to top. Adjust the diameter and height along the way and fasten the circles with a cross lashing. The basket should be as high as your back. You can measure it by sitting next to the pack on the ground. It should reach no higher than your shoulders.

Now that you have the bones of your basket, you can now weave cord or rawhide into a net formation in the spaces between the branches and mount a carrying system like on the other backpack frames.

GLUE

Tools: Knife, can.

Glue from resin has been used as far back as the Stone Age, for example, to glue arrowheads on arrows. In order to produce strong and durable glue, you have to mix fibers and bulk into the resin.

Start by collecting resin, which can be found on all conifers, though pines are the ones with the most resin. Resin is a turpentine-containing substance that conifers produce as a kind of wound scab to close any damage to the tree or bark. Therefore, also look for damage to the wood when looking for resin. Carefully break the resin lumps off the wood with a knife or pointed stick.

Also, collect dry grass or excrement from deer, as both contain a lot of fiber. Collect some ashes from the bonfire and find a metal container that can be used to heat and mix the glue.

Carefully heat the resin, being careful not to overheat it.

When the resin has a slightly fluid consistency, mix in the ashes and animal excrement or finely chopped dry grass. Take the resin off the fire.

When the glue begins to cool but is still malleable and not too hot to handle with bare hands, knead it into a lump and put it on a stick for future use.

When the glue is to be used, carefully reheat before applying to your object of choice.

NET NEEDLE

Tools: Knife, possibly saw.

Using nets for fishing is an ancient method that dates back to at least eight thousand years ago. The oldest net to date was found in Kamennogorsk, Russia.

In order to make a net, you don't actually need anything other than some suitable cord. However, it makes the process much easier and more precise by using a few simple tools, such as a net needle and a gauge. A net needle is a holder for the cord from which you want to tie your net. The net needle makes it easy to pass the cord through the mesh of the net and tie it

correctly. The gauge or mesh gauge is used to ensure that the mesh in the net is the same and equal in size.

To make a net needle, you must use a suitable piece of wood, such as ash or pine. Start by splitting the wood so that you end up with a flat piece of around ⅕–⅜ inch (5–10 millimeters). Then, draw your net needle on the wood in the desired size. Be careful not to make the net needle too large, as it needs to be able to pass through the mesh while making the net.

Now, make as deep a cut as possible along the inner edge of the line for the net needle, then carve away material by making a 45-degree cut to the line. In this way, you can remove material in a controlled and careful manner without damaging the net needle itself. Continue removing material like this until you get all the way through the wood, after which the inner part of the net needle can be carved cleanly and neatly into the shape of the net needle pictured on the previous page. It may be necessary to carve from both sides of the net needle if it's thick enough. Be careful not to break off pieces with the knife, as

you risk breaking the edge or center of the net needle.

When the hole in the center of the net needle is carved clean, you can shape the outside of the net needle. If you start with the outer part of the net needle, you weaken the needle before you carve the middle part, and there is a greater risk of it breaking during the carving process. When the needle is finished being carved and dried, it can be sanded nice and smooth with fine sandpaper.

Now, the net needle is ready to mount the cord from which you want to make your net. Start by folding the end of the cord so that it forms a small eye that can be pulled down the middle of the needle. Then, bring the cord down around the arch at the bottom of the netting needle and up around the needle on the other side, and continue like this, switching from side to side, until the net needle is full of cord. Now, the net needle is ready to use, but we still need our gauge to be able to make a net. A gauge is, in all its simplicity, an oblong piece of wood that has been carved so it's smooth and clean of irregularities with a width that is half as large as the desired mesh size of the future net. It can help to carve your gauge slightly cone-shaped in thickness, which makes it easier to get the cord off the gauge when you tie your mesh on it. (Read more about the use of this tool in the next project.)

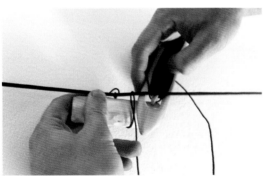

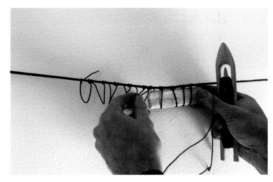

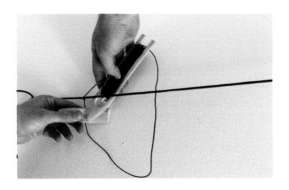

NET

Tools: Net needle, gauge, cord.

Over time, nets have been used for many different purposes, from fishing to storing crops and cargo. There are several

118

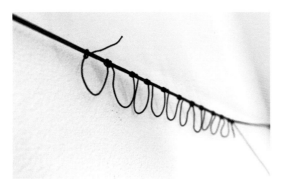 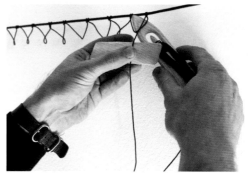

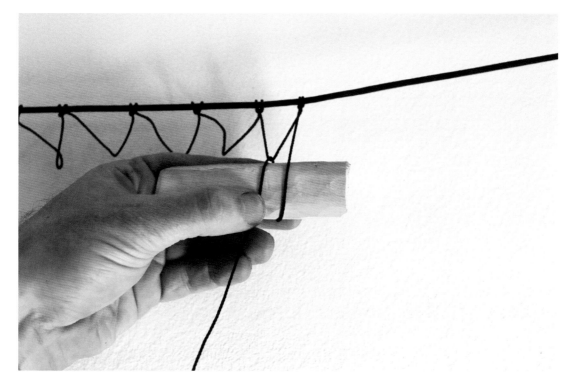

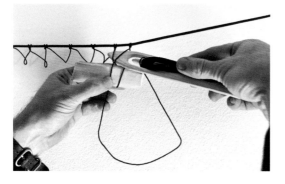 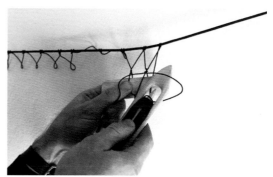

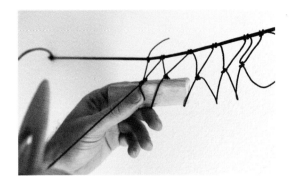

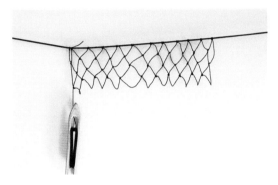

a small loop is formed around the gauge and the cord can be passed through and tied off on the horizontal cord. Continue like this along the horizontal cord until you have the desired width of your future net.

When you have reached the desired width of the net, hold the gauge up to the newly made mesh (half mesh) and lead the cord from the net needle on the front of the gauge, then behind and up through the newly made mesh (half mesh). Pull the cord tightly so that it is tight around the gauge and the gauge follows the edge of the newly made mesh (half mesh).

Now, pass the net needle and cord around the half mesh so that the cord forms a loop around the half mesh just above the gauge, then pass the cord through this circle to form a single knot and tie off the mesh. Continue tying off mesh from right to left until you end up where you started on your net. Continue to work with the net back and forth until the desired depth of the net is achieved.

If the net is to be used as a fishing net, it helps to mount something like branches on the horizontal cord at the top of the net and stones or similar at the bottom of the net so that the net can be kept tight and level in water.

different ways to tie nets. Here is the simplest procedure.

Start by deciding how long the net should be, then tie a cord, preferably a bit thicker than the net itself, between something like two trees. Next, take your net needle with wrapped cord and tie the end of the net needle cord to the horizontal cord with a single knot. Place the knot at one end of the horizontal cord.

Now, hold your gauge up to the horizontal cord and let the cord on the net needle fall down behind the gauge. Pass the net needle and cord up in front of the gauge and over and around the horizontal cord, first with the cord around the gauge and then once more without the gauge so that

OTTER BOARD

Tools: Ax, saw, knife.

An otter board—or planer board, as it's also called—is a fishing tool that is typically used when trolling with a boat to be able to fish a wider area. It is a small floating device to which one's fishing line is attached. The otter board is designed so that it drifts outward when you put it in water and give it a line. On the line from which the otter board drifts out, shorter lines are mounted with hooks at a suitable distance. That is, as the otter board drifts out farther and farther, you can have hooks in the water about every 10 feet (3 meters). The otter board works on calm water, both on lakes and from the coast, where it can drift out onto the water while walking with the line along the bank.

There are many modern models of the otter board, but here is an example of one that can be made from natural materials. To get the most stability in the otter board, you can make it like a small catamaran.

Find a log or a branch with a diameter of 2–2¾ inches (5–7 centimeters) and saw two equally long pieces of 12–15¾ inches (30–40 centimeters). Now, chop or cut an angle at one end of the logs at approximately 45 degrees. This is important, as the otter board will later use the angles as a form of rudder to steer it outward in the water.

Now, find a couple more branches or logs and prepare them to be tied on the otter board to form a square. Let the front log (in the sailing direction) extend 4–6 inches (10–15 centimeters) farther than the other, as shown here. It is important that this is done on the correct side.

Make a small groove at the end of the front and longest log that you can tie your fishing line onto. This gives a skewed pull on the otter board, which also forces it to sail out from the direction of the pull.

Now, you can mount your fishing line and attach extra lines and hooks to it at regular intervals, as on a regular long line. Feel free to roll up your fishing line on a small piece of wood so that it's easier to keep track of when using the otter board.

Now, the otter board is ready for use and really just needs to be put in the water at your desired fishing spot. Give an even pull on the line, and at the same time give more line as the otter board drifts farther and farther out on the water. You can now fish a large area directly from this width.

CORACLE BOAT

Tools: Saw, knife, ax.

A coracle is a small, simple boat that originated in Wales and has been used as a fishing vessel for more than two thousand years. The coracle is relatively easy to make from something like woven willow or hazel.

Originally, the wickerwork was covered with skin or canvas coated with tar. Similar boats have also been used elsewhere, like in Asia. Here, I offer instructions for a coracle made of hazel and covered with tarp.

Start by collecting approximately ten pieces of long, straight hazel sticks, and carefully bend a circle from one to two sticks so that the circle has a diameter

of 3–6 feet (1–2 meters). The circle is most easily made by placing sticks in the ground in a circle of the desired diameter. The sticks can help hold the hazel circle when it's shaped and tied together. Start by securing the hazel circle with a Canadian jam knot and tie it together with a whipping knot.

Then, bend at least four hazel branches into a bow and tie them on the circle at a suitable distance so that it forms a dome with a height of approximately 1½ feet (½ meter). Then, add at least four hazel branches across the first four and tie them together with cross lashing where they overlap each other.

When the whole skeleton is finished, spread the tarp out on the ground and cut

to approximately 4 inches (10 centimeters) larger than the shape of the skeleton. Now, sew the tarp on the outside of the skeleton by wrapping the tarp over the edge of the skeleton and sewing it under and over the edge of the skeleton with a strong needle and thread.

If you want a seat in the boat, before mounting the tarp, mount a board as a seat with a few holes at each end of the board that can then be placed in tension between the hazel branches. Now, all you need is a paddle and you're ready to hit the water. Remember to wear a life jacket and be aware that this vessel is only suitable for still water.

BOUGH BOAT

Tools: Saw, knife, optional ax.

A bough boat is a simple craft that can easily be made in an hour or two if you have the materials for it. A bough boat is

made of a tarp that's filled with something like pine boughs, hence the name, and supported by a frame of logs. The tarp is then folded and tied up around the frame so that water can't enter the boat. When you sail in the boat, you sit on the frame itself. The filling of the pine boughs gives the boat buoyancy and can be made in different sizes, depending on how many or how much it needs to be able to carry. Most often, the boat is used to fish from calm water or to cross a body of water without having to get wet.

Start by laying out your tarp on the ground. Now, fill the tarp with something like pine boughs in a donut shape, until the pine bough circle has a diameter of at

least 3 feet (1 meter) and a height of about 6 inches (30 centimeters), depending on how much it needs to be able to carry.

Then, make either a cross or a square frame of logs to fit inside the size of the pine bough circle, and tie, if necessary, a cross brace or two on the frame. First use the Canadian jam knot, then cross lashing to tie the frame together.

Place the frame on top of the pine boughs and fold the tarp up around it so that there are no openings in the tarp. Now, tie the tarp tightly around the frame and you are ready for your maiden voyage with the bough boat. Use a paddle with the bough boat, and always remember to wear a life jacket and to follow applicable safety rules for sailing.

PADDLE

Tools: Saw, ax, knife, wood knife.

A paddle is a short oar typically used in a canoe. Being able to make a paddle from nature's materials can prove to be a life-saving skill, if you lose your paddle in the wild and can't transport yourself farther.

The paddle must not be too heavy but must also be strong and should be made of wood with long, strong fibers, like pine, ash, or hazel. It can be made from one or more pieces of wood. In this case, it's made from two pieces that are wedged and tied together.

Start by finding two pieces of wood: one piece with long straight grain for the shaft and handle, and a wider piece with relatively straight grain for the blade. Now, split the piece that will make up the blade into a suitable thickness, approximately 1¼ inch (3 centimeters). Remember to split the trunk with equal mass on both sides of the split, so the wood doesn't run to the side.

Now, draw the desired shape of the blade and preferably use an ax first, then a knife to carve the shape of the paddle. At the top of the blade where the shaft is to be mounted, carve the blade to match the diameter of the other part of the paddle. Saw two notches approximately 2 inches (5 centimeters) deep at the top of the blade and carve away the material between the two notches.

Now, carve the shaft and handle so that you get a paddle that fits you and your hand.

The optimal length of a paddle for a canoe is found by sitting on the ground and holding the paddle upside down so that the handle is on the ground where you're sitting. The blade should reach the center of your face.

When the shaft and handle have been carved, measure the bottom of the shaft on the blade so it can be carved to fit into the notch you've made on the blade. When the two pieces fit together as well as possible, tie with a tight whipping knot and the paddle is ready for use.

If you have access to sandpaper and possibly oil or varnish, you can sand, oil, or varnish the paddle so it doesn't absorb water during use and has better performance in the water.

If you can find one piece of wood to make your paddle from, you can avoid having a joint on the paddle. Here, the procedure is more work with an ax and knife, a bit like making a large spoon. Saw some stop cuts here where the blade becomes the shaft. This is done by sawing a notch, so that the cut or chop with the ax doesn't continue farther down the wood. First, use the ax to remove material, then the knife for the finer work.

WILLOW WEAVE

Willow weave has been known since ancient times. In the late Iron Age, willow was especially used for eel traps and wicker doors.

Willow grows very quickly and can be harvested every year during the winter months.

Before use, dry willow shoots must be softened in water to regain their flexibility. Place them in at least 60°F (15°C) warm water, making sure the entire willow shoot is covered with water. Leave them like this for at least a week. If necessary, check if they're saturated by occasionally cutting part of the thick end of the willow. When the willow is completely saturated, it's

ready for use. This process may be accelerated by adding hot water.

FISH TRAP
Tools: Knife, possibly pruning shears.

There are many different designs of fish traps that are woven from willow. Here is just one of many models. For this fish trap, you need an odd number of willow shoots, approximately 37–39 pieces in total at approximately 6½–7 feet (200–220 centimeters) each. In addition, you need 8–10 pieces to weave with and make the funnel from.

Start by carefully bending a willow shoot into a circle approximately 8 inches (20 centimeters) in diameter, depending on

how big a fish trap you want. Now, twist the ends of the willow shoot around each other so that the circle can hold its own shape. This circle will be the base of your fish trap, and this is where you attach the rest of the willow shoots.

Now, take a number of willow shoots and make a cut approximately 6 inches (15 centimeters) in length at the thick end of the willow shoot and cut approximately half the diameter of the thick end of the willow shoot away. Be sure to start the cut steeply so that an edge is formed that can later sit against the base of the lure.

Start weaving the long willow shoots on by laying the cut part of the willow shoot up to the circle so that the cut edge is close to it. Now, fold the cut end of the willow shoot around the circle and let it come up, around, and over itself so that the cut part of the willow shoot points diagonally either to the right or to the left. Holding it in place with thumb and forefinger, place a willow shoot at a suitable distance from the first on the circle and weave it in the same way as the first, over the end of the first notched willow shoot.

Continue this process all the way around the circle with your desired spacing. Be aware that the smaller the space between the willows, the less fish it is possible to catch with the fish trap.

When all willow shoots are mounted on the circle, they are temporarily tied together at the other end. Now, weave a number of thinner willows alternately above and below the willows mounted on

the circle to strengthen the structure of the fish trap.

Make one more circle of willows in the diameter that you want the fish trap to have in the middle. The circle is temporarily tied inside the fish trap. Then, weave some thinner willows on the other side of the center circle in the same way as before.

When the fish trap is firm and stable, the main part of the fish trap is finished. Now, a funnel must be made that's mounted at the top of the fish trap to ensure fish can swim into the fish trap, but not out.

The funnel is made largely in the same way as the main part of the fish trap. Start by making a circle of willow that fits into the circle on the fish trap and follow the same procedure as with the fish trap itself, with the one change that you need to leave the end open so the fish can swim in through the funnel. Attach the funnel to the fish trap with cord or a small piece of willow so that it doesn't fall out during fishing.

SIMPLE BASKET
Tools: Knife, possibly pruning shears.

A basket or container has had great importance for human survival and the possibility of being able to transport things like food, clothes, and tools from place to place.

There are many beautiful and creative ways to weave and just as many materials to weave with, like willow, blackberry, cattails, and hazel. Here is a simple and easy weaving technique with willow that can also be used with many other materials.

First, soak the willow (see "Willow Weave" on page 128). When the willow is ready for use, assess how big a basket you want to make, then cut six or more willows to the length you want the basket to be, including both the bottom and the two sides.

Now, place the willow shoots three by three so they form a cross. Take a thin willow and fold it in half and use it to secure the cross by folding it over and under the willows that form the cross. Do this twice around the cross and start separating into a total of twelve willow shoots. Weave the rest of the thin willows alternately over and under the individual willow shoots.

When you have used up the thin willows, take a new willow and cut the very thickest and thinnest part of it and continue weaving from where the thin willow ends, starting with the thin end of the shoot. Now, weave alternately over and under the shoots, making sure that your weave is tense and tight.

Once you have achieved the desired size of the bottom of your future basket, you can either start bending the willow shoots upward so that they begin to form the wall of your basket, or you can cut the excess of the willow shoots and introduce some new long willow shoots at the side of the original ones. The new willow shoots will then form the wall of your basket. Continue to weave the willow over and under the willow shoots, simultaneously pressing them upward, until you have achieved your desired basket shape and height.

Always leave 2–4 inches (5–10 centimeters) of the willow shoots to finish the edge. This is done by first sharpening them slightly, then bending a willow shoot perpendicularly over the next willow shoot and bringing it down into the woven basket wall again at the next willow shoot. So, you

Now, the basket is finished and ready to use. If you wish to add a handle to the basket, this can be done easily by taking two or more willow shoots, cutting them pointed at both ends, and running them down into the weave of the basket wall, first on one side, then twisting them around themselves and leading them down into the weave of the basket wall on the opposite side. Now, you have a simple and useful handle basket for storing or collecting things like berries or mushrooms.

jump over a willow shoot before running the shoot down into the basket wall. Continue like this with all the willow shoots.

When you've come all the way around, you will find that a willow shoot is missing to lead around at the end. Find the first willow shoot you completed and run the last willow shoot around it and down into the basket wall at the next one.

BOW DRILL

Tools: Knife, possibly saw.

There are many different techniques for producing fire by friction, but the bow drill, or fire drill, is the most common and easiest, albeit still difficult. The bow drill consists of four parts: a board, a drill, a handle, and a bow.

To be successful with the bow drill, you have to have a lot of details under control. The wood must be a light type of wood, like pine, willow, hazel, or basswood, and it must be completely dry. The bow must be of good length, and the bow string must be tight so that as much energy as possible is transferred from the bow to the drill. You must also ensure that you sit correctly and hold the bow and handle correctly.

Start by cutting the drill, board, handle, and bow as shown on the next page. Make sure to sharpen the drill well at the end that will go up into the handle. Here, there should be as little friction as possible, whereas there should be as much friction as possible at the opposite end, where you need to generate a temperature high enough to ignite the wood dust generated when you rub the two pieces of wood against each other.

The bow must not be flexible, as it easily makes the string slack, so choose a reasonably straight branch of a certain thickness and a good length, 16–24 inches (40–60 centimeters). If you don't have cord with you, a shoelace can also be used, or the cord can be made from something like pine roots, stinging nettle fibers, or elm bark.

Make an indentation in the board for the drill to grip to start with and drill the hole until you start to see dark brown or black wood dust around the drill. Put one foot very close to the drill hole and place one arm around the leg so that you can support the handle up your shin with your hand. Pull the other leg slightly behind your torso so you can make a regular sawing motion down the body with the bow. Carefully lean over the drill and handle so that you can use your body weight instead of your muscles to push down on the drill.

When you have drilled through the board and achieved good contact between board and drill, make a notch in the middle of the drill hole so that the wood dust has a place to collect and the opportunity to obtain so much heat that it creates small embers. Carve approximately $\frac{1}{8}$ of the drill hole away as shown on the next page.

Now, you're ready to make embers. Start drilling quietly, creating wood dust and heat. When the entire notch in the drill hole is filled with wood dust, it is time to generate so much heat that it forms embers. This is achieved by putting more pressure on the drill with your body weight and increasing the speed of the bow. Keep doing this until you run out of energy or until a lot of smoke and wood dust is produced from the bow drill.

With a little luck, you now have a little glow in the dust. You know when the dust continues to smoke after you stop drilling. Now, catch your breath and take it easy. You have plenty of time before the glow goes out, in fact it benefits from just growing a little bigger before you take it over to something like dry grass and blow it into fire.

FIRE BLOWING PIPE

Tool: Knife.

A simple tool to breathe life into the embers of a fire is a fire blowing pipe. It can be made from a straight branch from an elderberry bush, as elderberry has a soft, foamy core that can be easily removed. If it is constructed in nature, you can't expect it to be longer than approximately 14 inches (35 centimeters).

The fire blowing pipe can be hollowed out with a stick. Preferably, use a dry, dead stick as a drill, as a fresh stick will create more friction through the elderberry branch. You can also use a piece of strong steel wire, a baluster, or threaded rod as a drill by heating one end in the fire and burning through the core of the elderberry branch to achieve a longer blowing pipe.

A small, extra branch can be inserted into the end of the pipe to make it even more effective. You create a funnel shape, which results in more pressure on the air when it's blown through the blowing pipe, making it possible to have a longer and more targeted breath. The smaller stick should not have a hole size of more than ⅛ inch (4 millimeters) in diameter to work optimally and can be attached to the blowing pipe with resin glue.

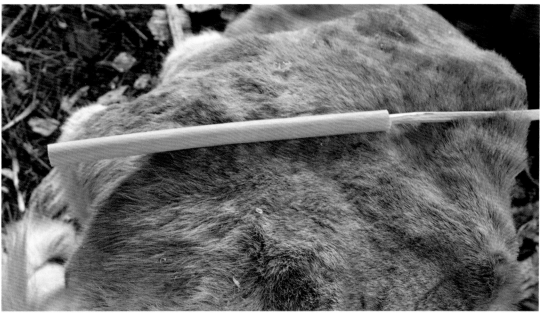

AMADOU

Tool: Knife.

Amadou is the outermost layer of the hoof fungus—a layer that, when fresh, can be shaped, pulled, and worked a bit like felt, and is used to make clothes, hats, bags, and to catch embers for igniting fire. Hoof fungus, or tinder fungus (Fomes fomentarius), lives on beech and birch trees and is known by its resemblance to a horse's hoof, with its grayish, hard surface. Hoof fungus is perennial and can exist for more than ten years.

On the underside of the fungus are lots of small tubes or pores that look like small holes. If you saw or cut the fungus, you can see that it consists of pores, surface, and a brown felt-like layer in between that can be used as a catching material for flint and steel.

Cut out the felt from the fungus, let it dry, and scrape it into a felted material. Use it in the same way as charcloth (see "Bushcraft Dictionary" on page 232).

If you want an even better product, it can help to boil the felt in water mixed with plenty of ash from the fire—half ash, half water. Pound it into flat pieces with a stick and let it dry. This is also called amadou and has been used in fire making for millennia.

When you need to use it, just tear off a small piece and use it in the same way as charcloth.

USE OF IGNITION MATERIALS

With charcloth or amadou, it is easiest to pull off a small piece and put the charred material at the end of the knife and strike the flint along the back of the knife until the sparks land in the material.

Once the sparks have caught the material, it's time to bring embers to flame.

This is best done by placing the glowing material on top of some dry grass or fine wood shavings and blowing it into a flame. Make a small bird's nest out of grass and place the material where you can imagine the egg would lay. Then, carefully squeeze the grass so that it makes contact with the material and hold it up 4–8 inches (10–20 centimeters) in front of your face. Then, blow gently until it takes hold of the grass, and blow more forcefully until the grass ignites.

FAT LAMPS

Tool: Possibly knife.

We all know the classic oil lamp made of thin metal with a small glass dome, where the flame from the wick and the oil in the container under the lamp burn in peace from wind and weather.

This type of oil lamp has a few hundred years behind it, but oil—or, rather, fat lamps—in a simpler form have been found in various archaeological excavations and can be traced back four thousand years. Among other things, the Birka lamp originates from the Viking Age, and is named after the city of Birka, which we know today as Stockholm.

Common to these lamps, regardless of age, is that they all have some kind of holder that contains the fuel—fat, tallow, or oil—and a wick that can absorb the fuel and act as a catalyst for the fuel.

You can make such a lamp yourself quite simply if you have a container of fuel, which can be cooking oil, excess fat from cooking, or, of course, ordinary lamp oil. In addition, a wick of absorbent organic material must be used. Here, a piece of cotton fabric from an old T-shirt works just fine. You can also use materials directly from nature, like the pith from light reeds or dried moss.

THE BIRKA LAMP

The Birka lamp differs from the other fat lamps by having a small elevation in the middle of the bowl that contains the fuel. The elevation in the middle of the bowl is made to give the wick a support point so that one end of the wick can be raised above the fuel and thus ignite and burn in the middle of the bowl.

The bowl of the Birka lamp is made of ceramic, which is subsequently dried and fired at a high temperature in a fire. The bowl can be made easily from a small lump of clay, which is shaped into a small bowl with an elevation in the middle.

It is important when working with ceramics to be fired that they have a smooth surface without cracks and impurities like small stones, twigs, or leaves, as these create a high risk of the object exploding during firing. When the lamp is completely dry after a few days, depending on size and density, it can be fired in the fire. (See more about this in the "Ceramics" section on page 216.)

The Birka lamp can also be carved from soapstone or wood, which can burn if you're unfortunate, but all three types work excellently.

GREENLAND TALLOW LAMP

The Greenland tallow lamp originated in West Greenland more than four thousand years ago and was typically made of soapstone with a moss wick. As fuel, blubber from whales or seals was used.

This lamp has a different and simpler design than the Birka lamp, and is, in all its simplicity, an oval bowl with a side on which the wick can rest without drowning in the tallow. The lamp can be made of ceramic, soapstone, or wood. If you make it out of wood, it's a good idea to let the wick rest on a small, flat stone, so it doesn't have direct contact with the wood.

These lamps have a very simple design and can also be made from more modern materials like a canned food can or beer can, as long as you have a container for fuel and a place where the wick can rest without disappearing completely in the fuel.

CANDLE HOLDER

Tools: Saw, knife.

Making a candle holder is a fairly simple project that just requires a stick, some bark, and, of course, a candle. It can be a cozy detail, especially after dark, when it gives you the opportunity to sit and work on small projects after nightfall.

Start by finding a stick with a diameter of ¾–1½ inches (2–4 centimeters) and a length that approximately fits the desired height of the candle holder. Now, carve one end so that it can sit in the ground, and use your knife to cut a groove in the other end of approximately 2 inches (5 centimeters).

Then, cut a piece of bark ½–¾-inch (1–2 centimeters) wide and at least 4 inches (10 centimeters) long. Fold it in half and push it down into the groove on the stick so that it forms a small loop where the candle can sit securely.

Now, all that remains is to make a small wind screen that can protect the candle from wind and reflect the light in the desired direction. Here, take a larger piece of bark and cut a groove in it so it can be pushed over the bark that holds the candle.

If you want a candle holder that can stand on something like a table or similar, it can be made easily by using a branch with a large diameter that's sawed flat at the bottom and optionally fitted on both sides with candle holders made of bark. If you have a Scotch eye auger, you can, of course, also make one by sawing a piece of wood with a diameter of at least 2 inches (5 centimeters) and the same height, and drilling a hole in the middle of it that can hold the candle.

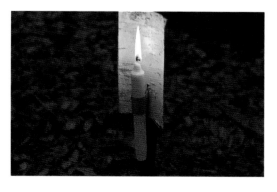

142

CLAMP

Tool: Knife.

A clamp can be a good piece of equipment if you need to be able to hold something firmly, like tension on a tarp that doesn't have an eye in the desired place.

First, find a branch with a diameter of ¾–1½ inches (2–4 centimeters) and a length of 2 inches (5 centimeters). Now, split the branch lengthwise, and possibly cut a few grooves in one end of the clamp to give it a better grip on its material.

Now, find the middle of the clamp and cut either a groove in both halves of the clamp or a groove in one and a ridge in the other. If you choose to make the clamp with a groove in each part, you must also use a small stick that can lie in the groove and give the clamp a tilting function.

Now, tie a tight lashing around the clamp so the two half branches and possibly the small stick are held together. Then, make a wedge that can be hit into the end of the clamp and cause the front of the clamp to clamp together and hold firmly onto the desired material. If you need to attach a cord to the clamp, it can be inserted from the front of the clamp to hold it in place.

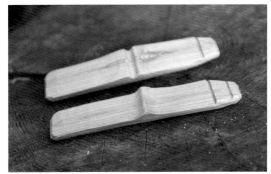

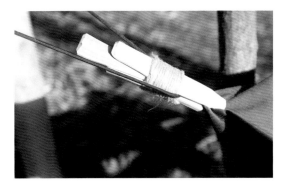

LADDER

Tools: Saw, possibly knife or ax.

No one knows for sure when the ladder was invented, but the earliest evidence of the ladder's invention can be seen in Valencia, Spain, in a cave painting that is about ten thousand years old and shows two men using a ladder to reach a beehive, presumably to gather honey.

If you need a ladder on your way through the wilderness, or perhaps on your hunt, it can be made easily with the help of a saw, some cord, and nature's resources.

Start by finding and sectioning off two logs or branches to the length you

want the ladder to have. Then, find a set of shorter logs to use as steps.

Now, lay the two long logs on the ground with a suitable gap corresponding to your desired width of the ladder, and find the center of your cord. Then, tie a double half hitch at the top of each log, but do not

cut the cord; leave it connected between the logs.

Now, pull the cord down along the logs, and where you want a step, run the cord around the log, over itself, and farther down the log. Continue this process until you reach the bottom of the logs, then tie off the cord with yet another double half hitch.

Push the steps inside of the knots you've made along the logs, then set the ladder up where it will be used. When you step on the steps, the pressure from your body weight should tighten the cord, and thus the steps, so that the ladder becomes safe to use. The cord at the top will help provide stability.

SHELTERS

Tools: Saw, knife, ax.

Being able to build shelter for wind and weather is at the top of the priority list when you're in the wilderness, regardless of whether you use a tent, a tarp, or nature's materials.

LEAN-TO SHELTER

The lean-to shelter is, as the name suggests, a shelter or half roof that leans on something, in this case a log or branch that is fixed between two trees. It is important that this log is solid and strong, as it must hold the weight of the entire shelter, which can become quite heavy, especially in wet weather. Choose a region where there is an abundance of materials for this shelter.

To avoid tying the lintel to the trees—and thus, over time, damaging the trees—you can use gravity and saw two logs to the desired height of the shelter, line them up against the trees, and simply lay the lintel on top of them. When you first start to lay the logs up against the lintel, it is held in place by the weight from them, and you therefore completely avoid having to tie it.

Depending on which region you are in, you can build the shelter with pine logs, pine boughs, or moss, or you can build it with leafy branches with withered leaves or peat on them.

Start by collecting a lot of logs or branches and take the branches off. Then,

place them up against the lintel so they form a steep half roof with room to lie underneath. It is important that the half roof is quite steep, otherwise it will not be watertight if there is a lot of rain. Keep the logs close if you plan to cover them with moss or leaves. If you choose pine boughs, they don't have to be quite as close together.

Once you have made the roof structure, it's time to make the shelter waterproof and windproof, in this case with moss. If you use pine boughs, you should start from the bottom and lay them on like bricks so that they overlap each other. If you use withered leaves, at least 12 inches (30 centimeters) must be added to ensure that it will be waterproof.

A lean-to shelter works best with a fire in front of it. The shelter directly reflects the heat from the fire, and if you make a long fire in front of it, you can sleep in the shelter without a sleeping bag, even if the temperature is below freezing, as long as you keep the fire going. You can further increase this effect by building a reflector wall behind the fire so that the heat is reflected into the shelter.

This shelter is also good for staying in and doing different tasks, such as preparing food and carving wood, compared to other types of shelters, which are more suitable for just sleeping in.

DEBRIS HUT

A debris hut is a small shelter made from available materials and is really more of a sleeping bag than a shelter.

A debris hut like this can be made by a single person in one to two hours if you choose a place with plenty of materials nearby. It's a fun project to do with the kids and can be a life-saving skill in an emergency, but due to the size of the shelter, it's not suitable for use on regular trips.

A debris hut is built around an A-frame with a lintel, and for that you need a long, strong log for the lintel and two branches for the A-frame. The A-frame can be made by weaving two Y branches into each other or by tying them together. For that, you need some cord, and you can find that in a forest by digging for pine roots.

Tie the A-frame together, put the lintel on, and measure the shelter so it fits for you to lie in it. It is important that it's not too big, so you end up with a small, closed shelter that can be heated by your own body heat.

Start building up the sides with dead, fallen branches. They don't have to be big and solid; almost anything can be used here. Before you finish building the walls, it can help to fill the shelter with a lot of leaves or pine boughs to make a soft surface to sleep on and to get up off the cold ground.

When the walls are finished, all you have to do is put a lot of leaves on top, at least 12 inches (30 centimeters), to make the shelter waterproof. The leaves are also insulating and help you retain your body heat during the night. It can help to use a Y branch as a rake to gather the leaves together. Start from the bottom, loading leaves, and work your way up to the top.

If you have access to making a fire and to finding some stones—not flint—you can dig a hollow in the front end of the shelter, heat the stones in the fire, tilt a little of the shelter aside, and put the hot stones into the hollow before you go to bed. Now, you have a shelter with heat, and you will be able to keep the heat even in freezing

temperatures, if done correctly. Remember to cover the front end well so that the heat doesn't disappear out of the shelter.

To make the entrance to the shelter, and to keep the heat in as best as possible, it's important that you can close the entrance well. The easiest way to do this is to fill a large bag with leaves and pull it in behind you. If you don't have a bag, you can make an entrance designed after the entrance to an igloo just by bending some fresh branches and putting them in the ground and covering them with leaves. Finally, collect a large pile of leaves that can be pulled in behind you and close the shelter completely when you need to sleep.

You now have a shelter that can save your life in an emergency situation in cold regions, made completely without tools, and from nature's materials.

SUPER SHELTER

The so-called super shelter was invented by legendary survival expert Mors Kochanski and works very well during the winter. The super shelter is lightweight and compact, and, when used correctly with fire, it can keep you warm without a sleeping bag on even the coldest nights.

The super shelter is made of a reflective back wall in the form of a space blanket and is closed at the front and sides with plastic, which can be anything from a plastic cover to garbage bags and your regular tarp. However, there is a risk of burning a hole in the plastic, as the fire is relatively close, so take that into account before using your expensive tarp for it.

This shelter functions as a greenhouse and allows radiant heat from fire to pass through plastic, where it's reflected inside and distributed throughout.

For the super shelter, you need:
- Space blanket
- Plastic
- Cord
- Tape

Start by setting up your space blanket as a lean-to shelter (see page 146) at an approximately 45-degree angle. Then, hang the plastic over the shelter and cut the sides so that they can be folded around the corners and taped to the back side of the shelter.

Make sure you have plenty of plastic in the front so that you can roll a log or branch into it and make the front even and tight. Use this log as an entrance to the shelter and easily lift it aside from the inside when more firewood needs to be added to the fire.

To heat the shelter, you must use fire, and to get the most heat out of it as possible, I recommend making a reflector wall behind the fire so that the heat is reflected toward the shelter and doesn't just disappear into the forest.

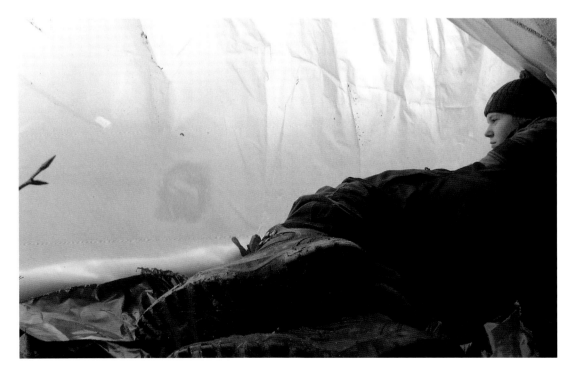

TEEPEE

The teepee is attributed to Native Americans and has been used for several centuries. The northern European version, used by the Sami people of Lapland and Siberia, is called a lavvu, and is slightly lower and wider to make it more resistant to strong wind.

The teepee is a brilliant construction, originally made of logs covered with skins and with the option of having a fire inside the tent so that you can keep warm in the winter and cook regardless of the weather outside. Today, teepees are typically made of logs covered with canvas, but can also easily be made with something like a cheap tarp from the local hardware store. The cover for a teepee is really just a piece of material in a semicircle that's tied up on the logs, pulled around them, and gathered at the front of the teepee.

To build a teepee, you need a large tarp or similar. Lay it flat on the ground and find the center of the long side of the tarp and mark it with a peg or branch. Now, using a cord attached to the peg, measure out a semicircle by measuring the length of half the long side of the tarp from one corner, around the tarp, to the other corner.

With a bit of cord around the curved part of the semicircle, attach the cords with a double half-hitch and a small stone, cone, or similar under the tarp and use the cords as guy-lines for fastening the pegs later. There must be approximately 3 feet (1 meter) between each cord, and the ropes should be 8–12 inches (20–30 centimeters) long so that you can tie a loop around them and fasten the tarp with the pegs.

The curved part of the semicircle ends up being the base of the teepee. Once the semicircle is measured out, you can cut away the excess material or simply roll it up and push it under the teepee when it is erected. However, a teepee works best with a fire if there is some draft around the bottom of it where the fire can draw in fresh air, as the oxygen in the teepee heats up and rises up and out of the hole in the top.

Now it's time to measure the logs to the right length. For a small teepee with a diameter of 10–13 feet (3–4 meters), you typically need 6–8 logs, where a large teepee with a diameter of 16½–26 feet (5–8 meters) needs 12–16 logs.

Place three logs, that will form a tripod and the structure of the teepee itself, at the widest point on the semicircle and let them stick out approximately 4 inches (10 centimeters) beyond the tarp. Now, tie the three logs together (as shown in the "Tripod" section on page 82) so that the binding is tied at the same length as the widest point of the semicircle + 4 inches (+10 centimeters).

Then, raise the tripod and pull out the logs so that they're stable with the diameter you expect the teepee to have. Place the rest of the logs between the three logs on the tripod in this order:

Do not put up the last and back log—the one opposite the door—but instead tie the tarp to it at the middle of the flat end of the semicircle. Roll up the tarp on both sides of the log and lift everything over to the log structure and put the log in place.

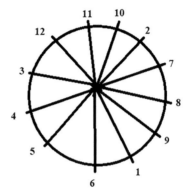

Then, roll the tarp around the log structure and tie it together where it meets on the opposite side. If there are eyelets in the tarp, these can be used. Otherwise, you can let the tarp overlap a little and tie it together with a small stone and double half hitch around both ends of the tarp. Leave a piece at the bottom open so there's an entrance to the teepee.

All that remains is to adjust the logs so that they stretch the tarp well, and put pegs all the way around. It helps to adjust the opening at the top of the teepee when making a fire, so you get the best possible draft and as little smoke in the teepee as possible.

You can also make a teepee only with nature's materials—this is most often

called a wiki-up, wigwam, or wetu, and has a more curved top than a traditional teepee or lavvu.

A teepee built from nature's materials is quite simple but time-consuming to make. Start by tying a tripod together in your desired diameter with something like pine roots, then lay a dense layer of logs all the way around. When this is done, and

you have made an entrance by tying a log across somewhere to hold the logs over the opening in place, all that remains is to cover the whole thing with a waterproof material like moss, pine, withered leaves, or the like. Leave an opening at the top for smoke from fire to escape.

GROUP SHELTER

A group shelter forms a frame for warmth, shelter, and activities in the cold part of the year. It is built as two lean-to shelters facing each other, with the ends closed and an igloo-like entrance added.

Start by building a frame for the shelter. This is done by using Y branches that are fixed in the ground in your desired size. Be careful not to make this frame too high, maximum 3 feet (1 meter). When the frame is built and stable, logs and branches can be laid at an angle of 60–70 degrees to the frame. Make sure a small opening is formed at the top of the shelter so that a fire can be made in the shelter afterward.

When the log walls have been built, it's time to seal the shelter, and here you can use different materials, depending on what you have available. It can be something like withered leaves, moss, pine boughs, or bark. However, make sure to apply a thick layer, especially if leaves or pine are used, so it forms a waterproof and insulating layer.

The idea of this shelter is to create an area under the slanted logs where you can sleep. At the same time, a fire can be made, and inside the center of the shelter is a living area. It can help to make an air channel in the ground to the fire to supply oxygen to it.

CABIN
Tools: Saw, knife, ax.

If you have your own forest or nature area, and you would like to create a more permanent place to stay, a log cabin can be a good option.

To build a cabin with a standing height of approximately 6½ feet (2 meters) you need around seventy-five logs, depending a little on the diameter of the logs. It is, of course, something you have to check whether you have access to in your area before you get started. You should only use dead trees for the sake of the forest, unless you have to thin them out anyway

to give space and air to the surrounding trees.

Start by building a skeleton for the cabin, which, in all its simplicity, consists of four corner posts and a frame for the roof. It can help to use some live trees in the terrain to attach the frame to. It can also help to start construction by attaching the front lintel to the roof between two trees, if possible. Feel free to let it rest on two logs that are tied firmly around the trees. From here, you have something to build on and attach the other corner logs to in the front of the cabin. The logs are not dug into the ground but are stable because one or more of the skeleton's logs are tied to a couple of living trees.

Attach two properly spaced logs—the logs should be 2–3 inches (5–8 centimeters) in diameter—at each corner so you can continue laying or tying between them all the side logs that will make up the walls. The technique is simple. The logs are laid horizontally between the two vertical logs at each end, of which the innermost vertical log is made up of the corner log in the cabin's skeleton. Tie the horizontal logs tightly together every fourth or fifth log. This construction technique can also be used when making a reflector for your fire.

If there's a need for more stability in the walls, possibly where the roof rises, an additional log can be tied on each side of the wall where necessary. If you want a

permanent roof and not just a roof structure that can hold the tarp that makes up the roof, you can lay logs next to each other across the entire width of the roof in the same way as with the walls.

When all the walls are up, you can start to insulate the cabin with moss or other material. This is done by stuffing moss between all the horizontal logs.

Finally, make the roof by stretching a tarp over the cabin. If you made the roof with logs in full width, when the tarp is installed you can put peat or moss on the roof to insulate it. Remember, there must be an overhang of approximately 12 inches (30 centimeters) on all sides so that the rain doesn't run directly down the walls.

CHAIRS

Tools: Saw, ax, knife, Scotch eye auger.

CHAIR WITH BACKREST

Being able to sit well after a long day is one of the things I miss the most when I'm traveling for a long time. Fortunately, there is an option for that, and there are countless options for building chairs and stools. Here, I offer instructions for making the chair that I think works best.

The bushcraft chair, as it has been dubbed by people around the world, is actually made from the same concept as the classic beach chair, and was further developed by my good friend, Søren Anker Nielsen.

It is, in all its simplicity, two triangle frames that can be pushed into each other and thus hold themselves and the seat you sit on.

Start by finding four strong branches or logs with a thickness of 1½–2 inches (4–5 centimeters). Then, cut the ends so that they fit together, two by two, and form two Vs with a distance between the branches at the wide end of approximately 16 inches (40 centimeters). Tie the ends together so you have two Vs. It can help to saw some small notches where the string is to be tied, to prevent it from slipping off.

After this, use a pair of crossbars of the same thickness. Now, determine the sitting height of the chair—typically, approximately 4–6 inches (10–15 centimeters) above the ground. Here, the two crossbars

must be mounted, one on each side, and with a gap not much larger than the thickness of the other V.

It is important to tie the crossbars correctly so that one branch sits on one side of the V and the other on the other side. Measure the thickness of the crossbars and cut them squared at the ends, if necessary, so they're easier to tie. Saw some notches into the branches where the crossbars will sit, then carve away the material between the notches so that the crossbars are easier to tie tightly onto the V.

When the crossbars are tied firmly, all that remains is to push the second V between the crossbars and make a seat to sit on. The seat can be made by splitting some branches or logs and placing them like a seat, or you can use some thinner,

flexible branches that provide a better suspension in the seat.

The chair is now finished and ready for many hours in front of the fire with a comfortable seat height and a backrest. The chair can easily be separated into two parts and taken with you on something like a canoe trip, where weight and volume don't matter so much.

STOOL
Tools: Ax, Scotch eye auger, possibly saw and knife.

A stool can be nice to have when, for example, you have to sit and cook by the fire or work at a chopping block. A simple tree stump can often be used as a stool, but if you want a lighter piece of furniture to move around, a stool is fairly easy to make with the right tools.

Start by finding a log with a diameter of 8–12 inches (20–30 centimeters), then saw a suitable length of approximately 16 inches (40 centimeters). Split it down the middle with the ax, then find a solid branch or log with a diameter of 1½ – 2½ inches (4–6 centimeters) and saw four legs to your desired length.

Now, use the Scotch eye auger to drill four holes for the legs on the rounded side of the split trunk. Pay attention to get the right angle so that the legs will have a good, stable width.

Then, carve one end of the legs so that they are slightly tapered and can be tapped into the drilled holes in the trunk and secured with friction. It is important here

not to use fresh wood for the legs, as they will have a smaller diameter when they dry and can become loose.

You can let the legs go all the way through the stool and fasten them on the top side with wedges by sawing a cross in the top of the leg, hitting dry wedges in, and sawing off the excess material. This keeps the legs firmly secure so that they don't fall out if you move the stool around.

Use this stool as a carving bench by drilling some holes in the stool with the Scotch eye auger and making some branches that can be put in. With the help of a couple of wooden wedges, you can fasten a work piece between the branches.

EASY STOOL

A more transport-friendly stool can be made based on the classic hunting chair (a tripod with a seat). In this case, the seat is made of thinner branches, but it can also be made of something like fabric, leather, or woven cord.

Start by finding three solid logs or branches with a diameter of 1¼–1½ inches (3–4 centimeters). Then, tie them together with a figure-eight lashing in the middle so that they form a tripod (read more about figure-eight lashing in the "Tripod" section on page 82).

At the top of this tripod, drill a hole through each log with a Scotch eye auger or knife so that you can pass a cord through all three logs and secure the shape of the stool when you sit on it. Feel free to use a three-ply cord here, which can be separated later to mount the seat.

Now, find a handful of thinner branches and cut them to fit the triangle that makes up the top of the tripod.

Then, separate the three-ply cord so that the thinner branches can be pushed between the cord and secured. Typically, five to seven thinner branches are used to make up the seat. Once the seat is installed, the stool is ready for use and can be easily folded up.

ARMCHAIR

If you want a reclining chair to relax in, that can, of course, also be made. For this, you need three logs of the desired length (the chair can be made in many sizes), a tarp, a hammock or wool blanket, and a piece of cord.

Start by tying two of the logs together approximately 8–12 inches (20–30 centimeters) from the top so that they form a bipod—two logs or branches tied together at one end.

Now, fold your fabric in half and tie the loose ends together with a knot or piece of cord. Optionally, put a small stone or cone into the fabric and tie a double half hitch across the fabric and the stone so that the two pieces of fabric are tied together. Then, attach that end of the fabric to where the tops of the two logs are tied together.

Place the last log crosswise in between the fabric so that the log lies inside the fabric and at the same time supports the ends of the two joined logs.

Stand the chair perpendicular to a tree so that the legs stand a little away from the tree and the joined end of the logs leans against the tree. Now, you can sit in the fabric, which will make up the seating surface and the backrest, and the angle of

the sitting position can then be adjusted by raising or lowering the transverse log.

If you don't have a tree that you can lean the chair against, this can be solved by making a tripod instead of a bipod from the start of the project, and using this extra log instead of the tree. The chair can therefore stand freely and be moved around as desired. You now have a comfortable armchair to spend the evening in front of a fire.

The advantage of this chair is that it is extremely comfortable to sit in and quick to make. The disadvantage is that it requires you to have a piece of fabric to make it.

KITCHEN TABLE

Tools: Saw, possibly draw knife.

A raised kitchen table with room to work makes a big difference to the comfort in a camp where you have to stay for several days.

Find two logs and a couple of trees with a suitable distance and diameter. Tie a log on each side of the trees at a suitable height, approximately 3 feet (90 centimeters). Then, put cut logs on all the way across, and you now have a good place to prepare food.

TABLE AND BENCH SET

Tools: Saw, knife, possibly ax.

If you have logs available, you can make a table and bench set fairly easily.

Start by tying two large A-frames of logs with two center logs at your desired height for the table and benches, as shown here. Now, find a suitable distance between the A-frames. This distance determines the length of the table and bench set. Attach logs as a tabletop, and benches to the overhanging logs. Simply attach the outermost logs and place the others in tension between them.

You now have a good place to sit and work or eat. Depending on the length of the table and benches, there may also be room for guests. If you want to take it a step further, stretch a tarp over the overhead logs at the top of the table and bench set and fasten it to nearby trees or directly to the table with guy-lines and pegs for a covered table and bench set.

BEDS

RAISED BED
Tools: Saw, ax, or knife.

A raised bed is one of those luxury projects that is actually quite underrated. If you are on a primitive trip without a good sleeping bag, it is really worth considering

spending some time on a bed, as getting off the ground and having the opportunity to lie on a flat surface makes a huge difference to your night's sleep. If you have easy access to the materials, it won't take more than 30 to 60 minutes to make, with a little practice.

Start by finding and sectioning off the number of logs you want to use for the bed. Make sure to make them long enough for you to lie fully stretched out. It is recommended to make beds with logs running lengthwise, as this provides better comfort lying down and requires a lot less work.

Then, find two logs or stumps that can form the legs of the bed. Place the two stumps approximately 5–5½ feet (150–170 centimeters) apart on the ground and place the logs on top of them. Logs are

often thicker at one end, so I recommend alternating every other one upside down, so you have better comfort lying down.

Finally, all that's left is to make four long pegs to hammer into each corner to hold the logs in place. It's good to drive the pegs down so far that they are level with the upper side of the logs, so you won't be lying on them during the night.

Now, you can either use a skin, small pine branches, dry moss, or similar insulation on the bed. It can also help to stuff dry leaves under the bed to prevent cold air from coming up under it.

RAISED BED FROM A BLANKET OR BAG
Tools: Saw, possibly knife or ax.

A woolen blanket can be super lovely to have with you on a trip. It is durable and can replace a sleeping bag in the summer and provide extra comfort around the fire in the winter, but it can also be used to make a bed with so that you are raised above the ground and have good lying comfort.

Start by building two tripods from logs of approximately 5 feet (1½ meters). Place these at 6½–8-foot (2–2½-meter) intervals where you want to sleep. Then, lay your

wool blanket on the ground and place two logs of approximately 10 feet (3 meters) on the blanket in your desired bed width.

Fold the short part of the blanket around one log, then the other end of the blanket around the other log, and over both the first log and the short part of the blanket. When you lie down on the bed, the blanket should be held in place by your body weight. Lift the logs and blanket onto the tripods and let gravity hold the logs and blanket in place on the legs of the tripods.

Now, you can gently get into bed and lay down in a comfortable bed that is raised off the ground. If you are traveling during the cold part of the year, it can help to fill the space between the folded blanket with leaves to provide extra insulation.

You can use garbage bags instead of a blanket by cutting the bags open at the bottom and pulling them over the logs and otherwise using the bed in the same way as with the blanket.

You can also put an extra log over the top of the three legs and use this to lay a tarp over. Then, you have both tent and bed in one.

TOILET

Tools: Saw, Scotch eye auger, knife.

Having a toilet in the camp may be a luxury for some, but it is a necessity if you go on many trips or use the same camp for a long time.

A toilet can be made in many ways, but it should always include a deep hole, preferably 2½–3 feet (70–80 centimeters) deep, so that it can be covered with soil thoroughly after use. It should also contain a place to sit, and here you can quite simply tie a log or strong branch between two trees and dig the hole just behind the log so that you can sit across the log.

If you have the opportunity, you can also make a slightly more comfortable toilet seat from a larger debarked Y branch. Drill a hole at each end of the branch with a Scotch eye auger and attach legs to it so that it forms a Y stool. The legs must, of course, be of a certain dimension and quality, and must be cut at one end so that they match the diameter of the holes made with the Scotch eye auger. The advantage of this model is that you sit on it better, more in the style of a regular toilet seat, and that it can be easily moved.

Whichever toilet model you choose, make sure that smaller animals cannot fall into the hole, either by covering it with branches when not in use, or by building a small fence of branches around it.

SWEDISH TORCH

Tools: Saw, Ax.

The Swedish torch, also called the Finnish torch, is not a new invention, but has recently become popular as a garden torch, and can be bought ready-made in places like hardware stores. Normally, making a Swedish torch requires a chainsaw—or at least a lot of energy to saw by hand—but a Swedish torch can also be made in a much simpler way with an ax and a little cord.

Start by finding a tree trunk 8–12 inches (20–30 centimeters) in diameter that is dead, dry, and without knobs and side branches. Then, saw a piece of the trunk 12–14 inches (30–35 centimeters) in length, and split the piece of wood into four pieces.

Now, saw a couple of ¾–1¼-inch (2–3 centimeter) notches approximately 2 inches (5 centimeters) from the bottom in the split side of the trunk, and chop away the sides of the split wood with the ax. Now, assemble the four pieces of wood again like when they were a whole log, but now with an open X in it. Tie the pieces of wood together with a rope around the bottom, and stuff the cross-shaped opening with kindling, like fatwood or birch bark, and light it.

A Swedish torch is a good way to make a controlled fire, is especially suitable for cooking, and works well with something like deep snow, as the bottom of the torch doesn't melt down through the snow until the very end.

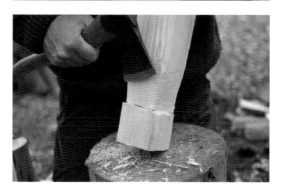

TORCH

Tool: Knife.

Torches have been around for pretty much as long as we humans have been able to make and control fire. They consist of a handle, a wick, and a flammable liquid or substance. In order to make a functional torch, one must first understand the principles of making fire. You can only make fire if the right conditions are present: oxygen, heat, and flammable material.

You need a handle for your torch, and it's often easiest to use a branch with a diameter of 1½–2 inches (4–5 centimeters) that you carefully split into a cross at one end, so it's possible to attach flammable material between the split parts on the branch.

Place some small branches in a cross at the bottom of the split part of your handle to make room for more material, and, where possible, tie a cord around the branch under the split part so that the splits in the branch don't run farther down.

Now, you need some combustible material like resin from spruce or pine trees. Resin contains, among other things, turpentine, which is flammable, but the resin itself doesn't burn very well until it gets really hot, so it needs a wick to work best. Small, dry pine branches or birch bark can be used for this purpose. When the space between the split parts of the branch is filled with resin and birch bark, the torch is ready for use.

Light the torch carefully, and if necessary, hold it horizontally for a moment until the fire takes hold of the material. You now have a torch that's easy to take with you and provides enough light to see where you're going or what you're working with. Depending on the wind, the material, and the size of the torch, it can last for 15 to 30 minutes.

If you have other materials available such as cooking oil, fat from cooking, and a piece of cotton fabric, you can also easily make a torch from this. Again, take a branch 1½–2 inches (4–5 centimeters) in diameter and fasten the cotton fabric around one end of the branch. Then, dip the fabric into the flammable material and light the torch. The fabric will now act as a wick for the flammable material, which is the oil or fat. When the torch starts to go out, it can be snuffed completely, and more oil or fat can be added to make it last longer.

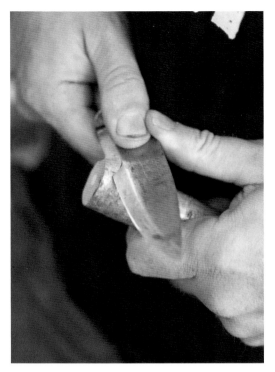

PEGS

Tools: Saw and/or knife, possibly ax.

The easiest thing is, of course, to bring pegs from home, but it is also quite easy to make them in nature.

Start by finding a solid stick that is approximately 1–1½ inches (3–4 centimeters) in diameter and 8–12 inches (20–30 centimeters) in length. Then, chop or carve to a point.

Carve the edges of the opposite end of the stick to help keep the stick from breaking and splitting when you hit it into the ground.

Now, saw or tap a cross in the stick with your knife approximately 1½–2 inches (4–5 centimeters) from the top. The cross must be approximately ⅓ inch (1 centimeter) deep. Now, carve away the three bottom triangles of the cross and leave the

last one on the stick to form a hook for the guy-line. Possibly cut a small notch under the hook so the guy-line fits better.

FIRE GRATE

Tools: Saw, knife.

There are many ways to roast a good steak or fish over the fire, even if you don't have a grill or pan with you. One of the easiest to control in relation to the heat is a grate for grilling made of fresh wood.

You need a green Y branch from a tree with long branches on the Y so that you can twist them around each other and make a circle with a handle. In autumn and winter, certain types of wood can be quite brittle and easy to break, so be careful when wrapping them around each other and string the branches around themselves first, if necessary, to make the wood fibers more flexible.

Then, put another branch along the handle up through the center of the circle. Now, weave smaller branches between the edges of the circle and the middle branch so that the whole thing will sit in tension and hold itself in place.

Use the grilling grate to put a steak, fish, or something similar on. It can help to fasten the meat between a couple of the transverse branches so that you can turn the whole grate instead of having to turn the meat itself on the grate. With this kind of grate for grilling, it's easy to control how much heat the food should have.

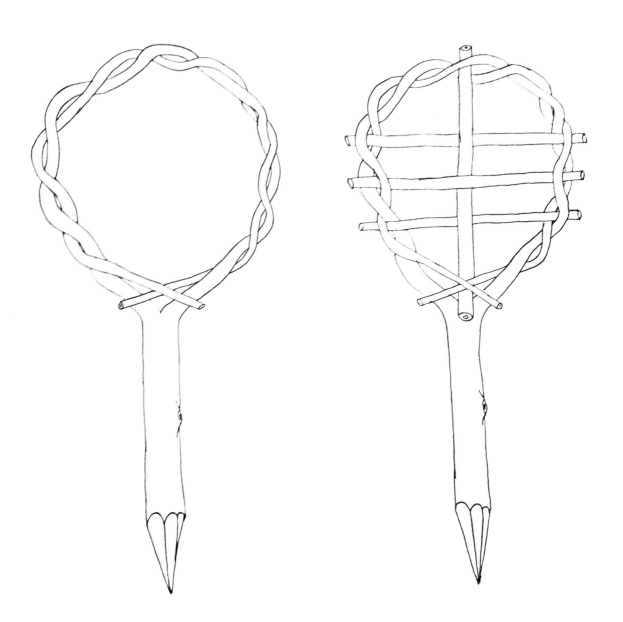

SAWS

Tools: Saw or saw blade, knife.

BUCKSAW

The saw is an important tool to take with you in the wilderness, but it doesn't need to take up much space or cost a lot. You can make it easily yourself in nature with just a saw blade, a little cord, and some skills.

Start by finding three sticks with a diameter of 1–1½ inches (3–4 centimeters). Two of the sticks must be approximately as long as your forearm, and the third should be slightly longer than the length of the saw blade. Now, proceed to saw or split the ends of the short sticks so that the saw blade can slide into the ends of the sticks.

Make two small dowels from dry, hard wood like oak or beech and insert them into the holes at the ends of the saw blade so that they can hold the blade later.

It is now time to mount the middle stick on the saw, and this can be done in several ways. The quick, but not quite as stable, solution is to cut the handles of the saw (the upper part of the short sticks) flat on the inside and adjust the center stick so that there is as much contact between the sticks as possible. Here, it is important to check that you make your cuts opposite the notches made in the stick where the blade is to be mounted. Otherwise, the saw will be crooked later.

A more stable solution is to saw an approximately ⅓ inch (1 centimeter) deep notch in the handles and carve away the

material between the cuts. The center stick can then be adjusted in length so it fits into the notches. Again, it is important to have as much contact between the two sticks as possible. It is this, along with how hard the saw is tightened, that determines its stability.

Now, make a couple of small notches on the outside of the handles at the top of the saw for the cord to lie in. Pick up the saw on the ground in front of you and tie a cord all the way around the handles in a circle. Find a small stick that is slightly longer than the distance between the center stick and the cord and twist the stick around the cord to tighten it up. It must be very tight. The stick can now rest on the center stick and keep the string taut. This saw can be easily disassembled by loosening the cord, and is so easy to take with you in your backpack.

SIMPLE BOW SAW

Another simple saw can be made easily from a saw blade and a fresh, flexible branch from something like hazel, willow, or ash. The only disadvantage to this model is that the saw blade can become loose as the branch dries and lose some of its flexibility.

Find a fresh, flexible branch approximately 1¼ inches (3 centimeters) in diameter and, preferably, 6½ feet (2 meters) long, so you have some length to work with. Now, stand on one end of the branch and gently bend it until you have a bow in the middle of the branch that matches the length of the saw blade you want to use.

Tie cord in a loop around the branch to keep the shape of the branch. Here, it

inch (a couple centimeters) with your knife so that the saw blade can be inserted into both ends of the branch. Now, you need two dry, strong branches that you can carve and use as rivets in the holes at the end of the saw blade to hold it in tension between the ends of the curved branch. Place the saw blade in place at the ends of the branch. Remove the cord from the branch, and the flexibility of the branch should now hold the saw blade in place.

BROKEN FOLDING SAW

If you've had the misfortune of breaking your folding saw, there's no reason to just throw it away. You can still use the saw blade and install a new handle on it.

Find a suitable piece of wood like birch, alder, or ash, and cut it to your desired han-

is important that you tie it on the inside of the bow from where the blade is to be attached so that the branch holds its shape when you cut it to length. Possibly put a stick into the loop and tighten the branches further by turning the stick around so it tightens the cord.

When the ends of the branch are cut to length, carefully split the ends about an

dle shape. Then, split the handle approximately 2 inches (5 centimeters) down with your knife where you want the saw blade to sit. Carefully mount the saw blade and make a tight lashing around the handle where the saw blade is attached. Now, you have a usable saw again, but it can no longer be folded.

CONTAINERS

Containers date back to the Stone Age, when humans developed a wide range of methods and technologies, including the manufacturing of containers, first from wood, wickerwork, horn, or stone, and since, from ceramics. Containers were used for everything from cooking to storage.

SHRINK BOX
Tools: Saw, carving knife, Scotch eye auger, possibly gouge, croze.

The shrink box is a fantastic wood project that dates back to the Viking Age and has been an important utensil through the ages. The shrink box has been made in many different sizes and has been used for storing everything from sewing notions to spices, flour, berries, and nuts.

A shrink box works in such a way that you hollow out a fresh piece of wood until you only have a thin outer wall left. You then fit a bottom from dry wood into it, and when the fresh wood dries and contracts, it tightens around the bottom, and you have a canister.

Start by finding and sawing a piece of fresh wood in your desired size. If you want to leave the bark on the finished canister, choose a piece of wood without too many irregularities and with a nice bark. Here, birch would be an obvious choice.

It can help to saw a thin, approximately 1/3-inch (1-centimeter) slice of your trunk

that can later make up the lid to the canister. This way, the canister itself and the lid will fit perfectly together. Now, use your Scotch eye auger to drill out the center of the trunk. Drill all the way through the trunk and use a long carving knife or gouge to carve away material until you have approximately a 3/16-inch (5 millimeters) edge left. Be aware that some types of wood have a thicker bark than others, so if you remove too much wood material you may end up with only the edge of the bark left.

When you have an even and neatly carved tube, you're ready to continue working on the bottom. For this, you need a piece of dry wood that has been split lengthwise along the grain and cut thinly and evenly. Place your canister on top of

the bottom and mark the shape of the canister from the inside by drawing it on the bottom. Carve the bottom of the canister so that it fits inside the canister. Be careful not to carve off too much. Better to take it a little at a time and adapt it along the way. Finally, carve the edge of the bottom so that it takes the shape of a knife's edge.

Make a small groove approximately 3/16 inch (5 millimeters) up from the bottom edge of the canister that can catch the bottom of the canister. This can be done with a special tool, called a croze, which is a small, V-shaped gouge. You can also easily, and with a little caution, carve the groove with an ordinary carving knife. Adjust the two pieces of wood (the tube and the bottom) to fit together as closely as possible, then

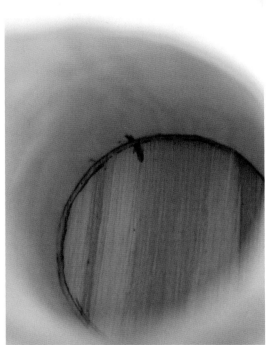

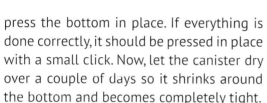

press the bottom in place. If everything is done correctly, it should be pressed in place with a small click. Now, let the canister dry over a couple of days so it shrinks around the bottom and becomes completely tight.

You already sawed a slice of the trunk that fits as a lid for the canister, but if you want a lid that sits securely on the canister, use this little trick: find a small, extra piece of dry wood that can make up an extra edge under the lid so that it's held firmly on the top of the canister. Start by filling the canister with some flour or similar and turn it upside down on top of the extra piece of wood for the lid. Then, remove the canister and carefully draw along the edge of the mark left by the flour. This way, you get a lid that fits perfectly on the canister. Now, carve the extra piece of wood so that it follows the outlined shape of the canister.

Fit both the lid and the extra piece of wood to match the rest of the container and attach the lid and extra piece of wood to each other by drilling a small hole in the middle of both pieces of wood and tapping in a wooden wedge, piece of bark, or pine root. It can also form a small handle on the lid at the same time. If you wish, you can, of course, also glue the two pieces of wood together.

To ensure that the handle doesn't fall out over time, split the wedge on the underside of the lid that holds the two pieces of wood together and hit an extra small wedge into the split wedge. This way, the wedge is kept in tension.

Another way to make the lid is by carving two tabs on the edge of the canister, then carving a lid with two ears that fit down into the two tabs on the canister. You can possibly drill a small hole through the edge of the canister and into the lid so that you can put a small wedge in the hole to hold the lid in place.

SÁMI NEEDLE CASE
Tools: Knife, Scotch eye auger.

A Sámi needle case, as the name suggests, originates from the Sámi in Lapland, who are reindeer herders and very naturally use meat, skin, and bone from reindeer. In many cases, they use the antlers to make containers that can be worn around the neck or a belt, in which you could have a small sewing kit.

This needle case is made of wood, as it is more accessible to most people, but if making this case with bone and antler, use a file rather than a knife to work the material.

Find a small piece of elderberry with a diameter of 1¼–1½ inches (3–4 centimeters) and a length of 3–4 inches (8–10 centimeters). Cut the bark off and hollow out the foamy core from the wood to make a small tube. Feel free to carve the inner part of the tube cone-shaped at both ends so that it's easier to insert the leather part for your sewing kit. Cut a small slice from the same piece of wood and remove the core from this as well so that it forms a small ring. It will later be used as a bottom to your needle case.

Now, you need a piece of thin leather that is approximately three times the length of your container, which is cut out as shown in the picture. Lead the leather in through the tube, and twist and tie the top together. You can even put a pearl on top, if you wish. At the bottom, tie or sew the wooden ring to the leather. Pay attention here to fit the top and bottom so that the middle of the leather, where your sewing kit is stored, can

be pulled completely out of the container for easier access.

Now, you can tie a leather cord at the top and wear it around your neck or attach it to your belt. True to tradition, you can make different patterns in the small container using kohlrosing to give the container a personal touch (read more in the Kohlrosing section on page 199).

BARK CONTAINER
Tools: Knife, saw, possibly awl.

The bark container is not a new invention. Throughout the ages, humans have used bark containers to store all kinds of small things, and the containers have been found in many shapes. Here, I will show you how to make a small, simple birch bark container with a wooden base and lid for things like spices, matches, and fishing tackle.

To start, you need a piece of bark without too many irregularities and holes. Clean the bark of fibers and impurities by scraping it with your knife at a 45-degree angle. After, cut the bark clean at the edges in a square. Then, draw an arrow as shown in the picture and carefully cut it out of the bark.

Roll up the bark to the way you want the container to look and mark the place where the edges of the arrow are on the container. Cut a groove in the bark at the marked spot, preferably $\frac{1}{16}$ inch (1 millimeter) or two shorter than the width of the arrow. Now, carefully insert the arrow into the groove so that the bottom of the arrow holds the bark in place in your desired shape.

Find a dry branch and carve it into a cone shape so that it fits the bottom of the container and cut off the excess wood. Here, it can help to use a little heated resin on the edge of the bottom to glue it firmly to the bottom of the container.

Now, make the lid for the container in the same way, but without gluing it in place, as it must, of course, be possible to take off and on. If you want a small handle for the lid, you can remove the center of the pith in the lid with an awl or a pointed, hard stick and make a handle from something like pine roots. The easiest way to attach these is to make a small wedge and tap it up between the roots at the bottom of the lid and cut away the excess material. Now, you have a nice little container for your small things.

There are countless different bark containers and designs that have been invented over time. Here are sketches of some of them for inspiration.

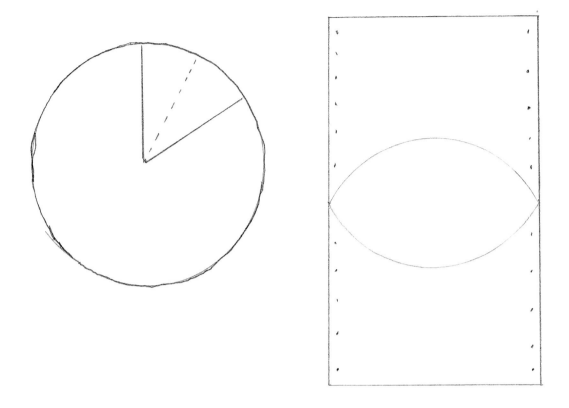

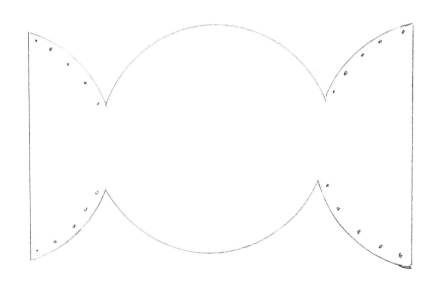

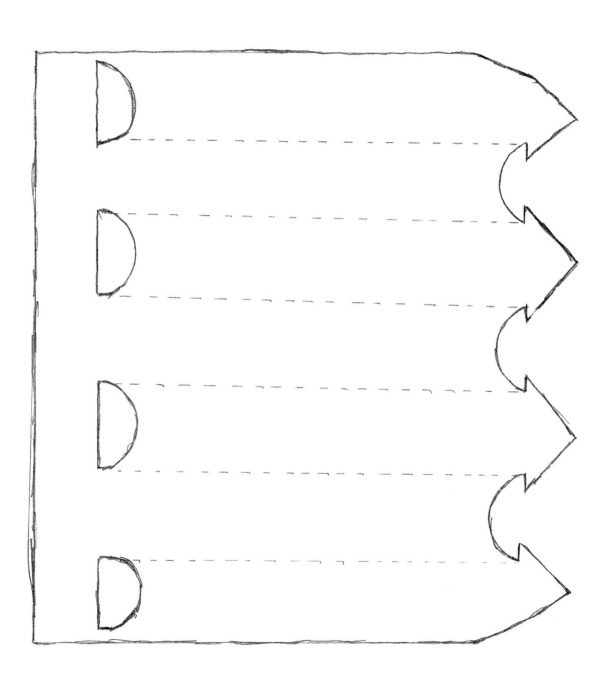

196

BARK SHEATH
Tool: Knife.

A bark sheath is an easy and quick way to make a sheath for something like a carving knife. The hardest part is typically finding a piece of bark that is long enough. You need a piece of bark that is slightly wider than the blade of the knife and four times as long as the blade. In addition, you need some bark to wrap around the sheath.

Start by measuring and cutting out the bark. Then, cut a thin strip of bark ³⁄₁₆–³⁄₈ inch (5–10 millimeters) or use a thin pine root to wrap around the sheath. Then, clean all the bark of unevenness and fold it, first in the middle, then at each quarter. Fold the outer two quarters into the

middle of the piece of bark, then measure if the blade fits in there. Take the thin piece of bark or pine root and wrap a full turn between the piece of bark from the bottom, then a full turn on the outside of the bark. Continue alternating between wrapping on the inside and outside. Make sure that it is wrapped slightly askew inside the bark so that it automatically wraps up toward the top of the sheath. Also, make sure to wrap tightly until you reach the top. Finish by cutting off any excess bark or root. Now, the sheath is finished.

BARK CUP
Tool: Knife.

The definition of a cup is a container that is waterproof and can be used to drink from, and this can be done in many different ways. One of these is with a piece of thinner bark, like birch bark, that has no damage or holes. It requires a relatively large piece of bark to make a cup this way, preferably 8 × 8 inches (20 × 20 centimeters) or larger.

Start by cleaning off the bark with your knife. Scrape with the knife at a 45-degree angle on the bark to remove loose bark and unevenness until the bark is reasonably smooth and clean. Now, cut the bark into as large a circle as possible and soak it in warm water.

Fold it approximately one-eighth over itself, so that the bark forms a cone shape, and use a small stick that you've split approximately halfway up as a clamp to hold the bark in the cone shape. You now have a cup that can be used to collect and drink water from. Note that the cup becomes quite soft if you drink hot drinks from it.

If there are leaks in the cup, typically at the bottom of the cone shape, they can be sealed with resin glue. (See the "Glue" section on page 114.)

BARK LADLE
Tool: Knife.

A ladle is a tool that has been used for centuries to serve soup, drinks, and stews, and is still used in the modern kitchen. A ladle is made the same way as the bark cup on the previous page, but instead of using a small stick to hold the bark with, you must use a longer branch of about 12–16 inches (30–40 centimeters) with a side branch at one end that can function as a hook on the ladle handle.

Follow the same instructions as the bark cup and split the longer branch that's used as a handle about an inch (a couple of centimeters) at one end and use it to hold the bark in the cone shape. To prevent the branch from splitting farther, it can help to make a whipping knot (see page 72) closest to the bark cup to secure the bark cup and prevent the split branch from splitting farther.

KOHLROSING

Tool: Knife.

Kohlrosing dates back to the Viking Age and is a traditional Scandinavian way of carving patterns in wood.

For kohlrosing, use a thin-bladed knife, like a carving knife. The thickness of your designs can be changed by either pressing deeply into the wood with the knife or adding light pressure into the wood with the knife. You can also choose to make a narrow V cut in the wood to get a thicker design.

Before you start, it's a good idea to draw your desired design with a pencil on the wood, first.

To give the design contrast, you can rub wet coffee grounds or ash mixed with a little water down into the design. Wipe off the excess color and gently sand the surface with sandpaper to remove any excess color.

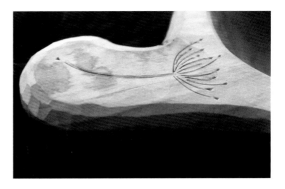

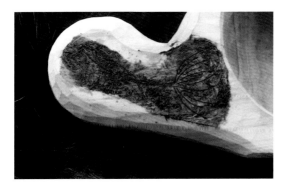

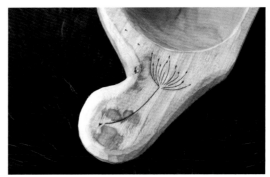

TONGS

Tools: Knife, saw.

A pair of tongs can be a nice utensil to have for something like cooking over a fire or for moving firewood or hot stones in the fire.

To make this model of tongs, you need two straight branches with a diameter of 1¼–1½ inches (3–4 centimeters). They should be as long as you want the tongs to be. Making good tongs has a lot to do with cutting at the right angles.

Start by carving the actual jaws of the tongs. This is done by carving one end of each stick so that they form a flat jaw facing each other. The flat part must have a length of 3–4 inches (7–10 centimeters).

Now, carve the handles of the tongs the same way, but at the opposite end of the tongs and on the opposite side of the branch.

Adjust the two branches so that they fit together by carving a straight surface perpendicular to the jaws of the tongs. About half of the sides of the branches should be carved away, and the jaws and handles should be carved to fit together.

Drill a small hole through both branches a couple inches (a few centimeters) behind the jaws with a drill or an awl. A small, cut-to-size branch should be mounted here that forms the hinge on the tongs. You now have a good stable pair of tongs to use by the fire.

WHISK

Tool: Knife.

A whisk is easy to make in nature and can be practical if you need to make gravy for dinner or perhaps whipped cream for Irish coffee around the fire.

Start by cutting the top of a small pine tree so you have the top itself and the first wreath of branches with it. Then, cut the branches clean of needles and bark. Bend the branches together toward the tree tip and tie them to the top with a whipping knot. Now, you have a nice whisk that you can add to your campfire equipment.

SNOWSHOES

Tools: Saw, knife.

It is believed that ancestors of the Inuit, and what we know today as Native Americans, emigrated from Asia to North America and brought along their snowshoes with them. At the time, snowshoes were little more than a few pieces of wood tied to the feet, but gradually they were refined into the ones we know today, with a frame of ash with woven rawhide.

Three different models of snowshoes were used as a starting point: the oval bear paw, which was mostly used in the woods; the long Yukon snowshoe, which was designed for powder snow in open areas; and the beaver tail model, which could do a little bit of everything.

EMERGENCY SNOWSHOES

If you find yourself in the wilderness and a lot of snow suddenly falls, more than 12 inches (30 centimeters), it can be incredibly hard and energy-demanding to walk. Fortunately, you can easily make some improvised snowshoes from pine branches with a little cord or webbing.

Find two wide pine boughs with dense side branches and saw them off where the branch is the same thickness as a little finger.

Lay the pine boughs on the ground and make a loop with your cord so that the loop goes around the branch, slightly in front of the middle of the branch. Now, place your foot so that the toe of the boot can enter the loop and cross the two loose ends over the boot. Now, pass the loose ends of the cord around the ankle and tie them into a bow at the front of the lower part of the shin or the shaft of the boot. You can possibly trim a little of the side branches of the pine boughs toward your legs to avoid stepping on your snowshoes.

You now have a pair of snowshoes that make it easier to walk on top of the snow.

ROYCRAFT SNOWSHOES
Tools: Knife, saw.

Tom Roycraft was one of the great icons of our time within bushcraft. He invented and gave his name to several functional projects, such as the Roycraft Snowshoes.

The Roycraft Snowshoes, or snow skis as they perhaps should be called, are distinguished by being very long and ski shaped. At the same time, they're relatively easy to make from existing materials and work incredibly well.

Start by finding your materials. You need ten long, flexible branches or shoots from a large pine tree with long side branches or a hazel bush. The thin end of the branches should be about the thickness of a little finger, and they should be approximately as tall as yourself if you are of average build.

Now, debark all the branches with the back of your knife or saw so that the branches dry faster and become lighter. When you have stripped all the branches, tie them together five by five at the thin end with a double half hitch, possibly with an extra knot to make sure they don't unravel. At the other end, approximately ¼ – ¾ inch (1 – 2 centimeters) from the thick end, make some small notches where you can tie cord, like paracord, around. To get some distance between the branches, tie three simple knots after each branch. Finish by tying a square knot.

Find the point of equilibrium on your snowshoes by balancing them on your hand. When you have found the balance point, mark it and tie a flatly cut branch to the same width you want the snowshoe to be. This is where your heel will come to rest when you step down on the snowshoe, as the vast majority of your body weight ends up on the heel when you walk.

Now, measure by standing with your heel on the branch where the next cross bar is to be tied. It should be tied on the snowshoe just before your toes, so your heel should be resting on a cross bar and the ball of your foot on a cross bar. Tie both of these cross bars on the snowshoe with a Canadian jam knot, possibly with an extra knot to make sure it doesn't come loose.

While the branches are still fresh and flexible, carefully bend the tip of the

snowshoes up so they don't dig into the snow as you walk, and tie them with a piece of cord from the tip with a double half hitch down to the first cross bar so they keep the ski shape. When the branches are dry, depending on the wind and weather, as well as the material, they should keep their shape, and these cords can be removed. However, the snowshoes can easily be used with the cords on. All that remains now is to tie them on the feet.

Using a strong cord, rope, or piece of webbing, start by making a loop of the cord around the center of the snowshoes and just behind the cross bar that will be under the ball of the foot, and bring the toe of your boot through the loop. Now, cross the cord over the boot, cross the loose ends around the ankle, and tie them in a bow at the front of the boot shaft or lower part of the shin. The reason why snowshoes are tied this way is to be able to lift the foot so that only the shoelace is attached to the snowshoe, because it gives greater freedom of movement.

SNOW GOGGLES

Tool: Knife.

Snow goggles have been used for approximately four thousand years to protect the eyes from the harmful UV rays from the sun. However, snow goggles have not always been fashionable with tinted glass and a wide band around the neck. Instead, they've been made of bone, antler, bark, wood, or leather, and have functioned in such a way that they had a narrow slit large enough to have a look through and small enough that not much light was let in.

Here is an example of a pair of snow goggles made from birch bark. Find and adapt a piece of bark so that it covers the eyes approximately ⅜ inch (1 centimeter) from the ears. Then, find the center of the bark and cut out a notch for the nose. Mark and cut out a strip by the eyes that is ⅛–¼ inches (3–5 millimeters) wide. Now, make a few holes with the point of your knife in the ends of the glasses so that you can fit and tie them around the head with cord or pine roots.

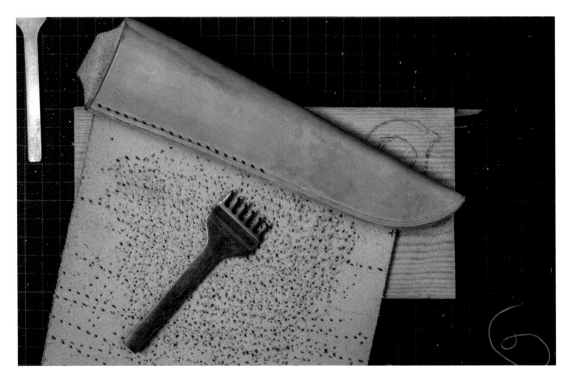

LEATHER

Tools: Leather tools.

Leather is a fantastic organic material that can be shaped and stretched. If you have gear made of leather and maintain it properly, it will last for many years, and it will only get a nicer patina.

Here, you will find directions for making a simple sheath for your knife and cover for your ax and maintaining your leather goods.

Vegetable-tanned leather is typically used for knife sheaths and ax covers, pressed front part, 6–6½ ounces (2.4–2.6 millimeters). It is especially suitable for knife sheaths that must be wet formed.

You can also use ordinary front part, 8–8½ ounces (3.2–3.4 millimeters).

To get started making leather projects, you need the following tools:
- Steel ruler, ballpoint pen, pencil, possibly a curve ruler and compass
- Hobby knife and extra knife (the leather is easier to cut out if the knife is sharp, so change the blade often)
- Stitch groover, 5-millimeter fork, size 1 edge beveler, diamond-shaped awl, punch pliers, riveting tool, and plastic mallet or rawhide hammer
- Needles and thread (either .8 millimeter or 1-millimeter waxed linen or synthetic thread like Tiger thread)
- Leather dye in desired color and water brush (or homemade fabric dabs)

- Wood burnisher or a smooth piece of nylon or wood for polishing edges
- Leather grease for care of the gear.

Use the following technique when you want to make a project with leather. Start by drawing a sketch of your project, then set measurements on the drawing and, if necessary, make a template on paper or cardboard. This gives you both the opportunity to test whether the project works and in what order it should be made. The subject should be drawn on the flesh side of the leather and cut out.

Now, make holes for rivets and snaps, stitch grooves, and stitch holes with the 5-millimeter fork. Be careful to keep the fork straight, otherwise you risk the stitching on the back becoming uneven. When there are more layers of leather, as with knife sheaths and ax covers, the sewing holes are not punched all the way through, but here a diamond-shaped awl is used at the end. Trim the edges where possible. On sheaths, the edges should be trimmed first, then glued, sewing holes should be punched, the edge straightened, and a finish should be made at the end.

If the leather is to have a different color, now would be the time to dye it. When the color is dry, polish the edges in the places to be sewn, like on belt loops on knife sheaths.

Using a saddle stitch, two needles on the same thread, start at one end and back stitch so you get a double stitch, then sew by bringing one needle in from the front and the other from the back of the leather. Tighten the thread with a light pull. To get a nice seam, you must use the same pull every time you tighten (it takes a little practice).

In some cases, the leather is glued together before being sewn for better durability. The glue should be applied to both parts being glued together. The glue must also be so dry that it does not stick to the fingers before you assemble the parts.

When everything is sewn together, the final edges should be polished. Give the leather a good leather grease and let the grease absorb into the leather overnight, after which the leather should be polished either with a soft cotton cloth or shoe brush.

If you take care of your leather goods, they will last for many years, and the patina will only get more beautiful with time. Do not store your leather goods in a damp place because you risk them becoming moldy. Take the knife or ax out of the sheath or cover when you get home from a trip so that the leather can dry. If the leather has become really wet, let it dry at room temperature and give it a coat of leather grease when it is dry.

Leather is a very flexible material, and a knife sheath will loosen over time. You can make it fit again by making the sheath wet in lukewarm water and leaving it to dry. The leather will shrink as it dries.

SIMPLE KNIFE SHEATH

This type of knife sheath is a friction sheath. In other words, its fit is tight, and the knife sits deeply in the sheath and therefore does not fall out. The sheath is folded around the knife. The construction of this sheath is made up of the following parts: the sheath, belt loop, and welt.

Draw a center line on a piece of paper. Place the knife with its back along the

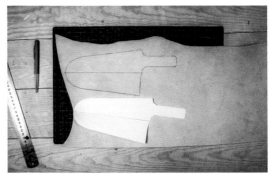

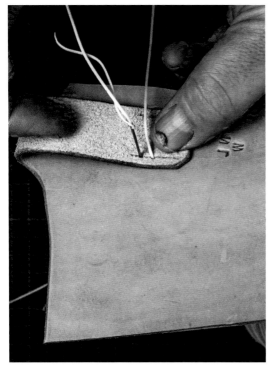

center line and mark how far up the sheath should end. Now, carefully roll the knife over on its side, without it moving, then draw the outline of the knife. Remove the knife. To make room for the welt, I add ⅜ inch (10 millimeters) to the outline and ½ inch (15 millimeters) to the top of the sheath. Now, you can draw the belt loop.

Typically, I make the loop to fit a 1½-inch (40-millimeters) wide belt.

Fold the template along the center line and cut it out. Now, the template is ready for use and can be drawn on the leather. Remember that the belt loop must face the right way, depending on whether it is to be a right- or left-hand sheath.

Holes for rivets and snaps are often made slightly larger than they will be, so things can be adjusted a little better when things have to be assembled. To make holes, use either punch pliers or a punch pipe. For stitching grooves, place a stitch groover approximately $\frac{1}{16}$–$\frac{3}{16}$ inch (4–5 millimeters) from the edge of the leather, and take your time, because you can easily cut crookedly if you go too fast.

If the leather is to have a different color, it should be dyed now. When the color is dry, the edges should be polished in the places that need to be sewn first, like the belt loop on knife sheaths.

Then, sew everything together, always with a saddle stitch, where two needles are used on the same thread. The thread should be five times the length of the stitching when it is for a sheath with three layers of leather.

After that, it's just a matter of sewing by putting a needle at each end of the thread and inserting one needle from the front and the other from the back of the leather.

Tighten the thread with a light pull. To get a nice seam, you must use the same pull every time you tighten (it takes a little practice). Secure the stitching by backstitching a few stitches, cutting the thread on the back, and burning the ends with a lighter.

When everything is sewn together, polish the final edges. Start by moistening the edges with lukewarm water, pure beeswax, or gum tragacanth, which is a gel that gives a nice finish. Polish with a wood burnisher or smooth object, like the handle of an edge beveler.

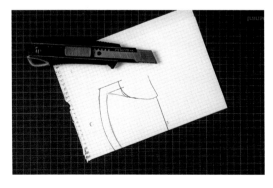

SIMPLE AX COVER

It is important to protect the edge on your ax with a cover. Avoid using rivets in ax covers, as they will damage the edge if you happen to hit a piece of wood with the cover on.

This cover is made up of the following parts: leather around the head, a welt, and a strap or leather lacing to secure the cover to the ax.

Draw a center line on a piece of paper. Place the ax with the top along the center line and mark on the paper how far up the cover should end. Now, carefully roll the ax on its side, without moving it, and draw the outline of the ax head. Remove the ax.

To make room for the welt, I add ⅜ inch (10 millimeters) to the edge. It is important that the cover is straight, otherwise you won't be able to get the ax into the cover.

Fold the template along the center line and cut it out. Now, the template is ready for use and can be drawn on the leather. See instructions as described in the "Leather" section on page 208. However, take into account that holes must be made in the cover for mounting the strap and snap or screw post.

Make the strap from the same thickness of leather as the cover and approximately ¾ inch (18 millimeters) wide. You can cut it with a strap cutter or by hand along a ruler. Make holes in the cover for mounting the strap and snap or screw post. Rivet the strap to one side of the cover and mount a screw post (use a little Loctite® if necessary).

The welt is made by placing the scored leather on top of a new piece of leather and marking it off. The welt must be ⅜ inch (10 millimeters) wide.

The cover can then be sewn together with a saddle stitch and finished as described on page 211.

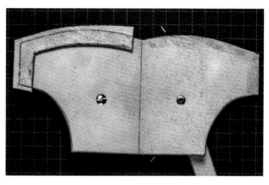

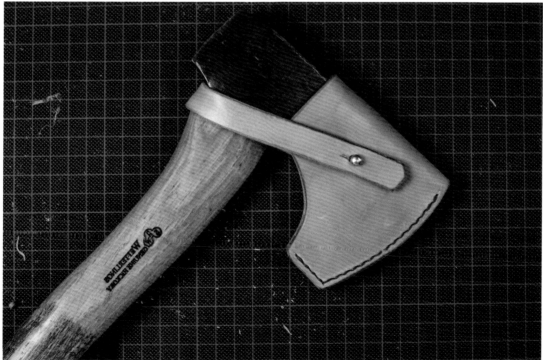

AX HANDLE

Tools: Saw, knife, ax, possibly draw knife.

Being able to make a new ax handle for an otherwise broken ax in the wilderness can be an important skill to have.

It is also important that the grain in the wood lies correctly to give the handle as much strength as possible. Choose a piece of wood that has the most straight and closely spaced grain.

Once you have found a suitable piece of wood, split the trunk out until you have a long, straight piece of wood of the desired diameter and length. Be careful to split the trunk so that there is approximately the same amount of mass on both sides of the split to prevent the trunk from splitting crookedly. You can use the broken handle from the ax to draw the new handle onto the piece of wood. Now, you can carve it to your desired shape with your knife, draw knife, and possibly a small plane.

It is important to let the wood dry completely before finishing the handle, as it

will decrease in diameter during drying. When the handle is dry, carved, and fitted to the ax head, saw a groove in the top of the handle where the head will be mounted. When the head is mounted correctly, hit a wooden wedge of dry ash wood into the groove, possibly with a little furniture glue smeared on the wedge so that it expands the handle and holds the ax head firmly.

CERAMICS

Tool: Possibly knife.

The use of clay and the ability to make ceramics is one of mankind's oldest artisanal skills.

Research shows that the properties of clay were probably found by chance. Before then, tight baskets were woven to fetch and transport water, and when you fetched water from rivers and streams, you also got some clay in the water, which was deposited inside the basket and hardened when dried. Along the way, people discovered the properties of clay and began to collect and process it directly from the ground.

In many places in the world, clay is rarely very far away. You can often dig it directly out of the ground or collect it from cliffs along the coast.

Clay is a fine type of soil with clay minerals in it and has good properties that make it malleable when wet but hard and breakable when dry. At the same time, clay can be fired at high temperatures, typically over 1,400°F (800°C), whereby it gains the ability to hold liquid, so that you can cook and bake in the pots you make.

If you collect clay from nature, be aware that it probably contains more than pure clay, such as pebbles and debris from trees and plants. This can cause the clay to explode or crack when fired, so it is

important to clean the clay before using it. This can be done in several ways. You can crumble the clay and let it dry completely, then sift it through a tightly woven mat or similar. You can also mix it up to a thin, muddy liquid, then strain out any impurities.

The following section shows you how to make functional and usable products without the use of expensive or special tools.

THE COIL TECHNIQUE

The coil technique is probably the best-known method for working with clay and involves rolling long sausage shapes of clay with your hands that you then shape on a flat base of clay.

The technique is as follows: start by making a flat base of clay with a thickness of ⅛–⅜ inch (5–10 millimeters) in your desired size. Then, roll sausage shapes of clay with your hands, and feel free to spread your fingers gradually as the sausage shapes get longer in order to get an even and straight pressure along the entire length of each sausage shape.

If necessary, smear the edge of the base with a little clay dissolved in water, called slip, to give better adhesion between the base and each sausage shape. Then, place each sausage shape around the edge of your base and press it on, carefully. Continue with all sausage shapes until your desired

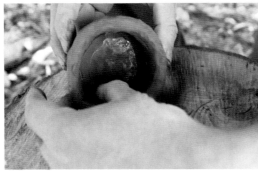

shape and size is achieved. Carefully squeeze the sausage shapes together with your forefinger and thumb to make good contact between them. If desired, the sausage shapes can be smoothed with a spoon or cut branch.

THE PINCHING TECHNIQUE

The pinching technique is a simple way to make clay containers if you don't have much experience. Start by taking a lump of clay and kneading it into a ball. Then, press your thumb down into the center of the ball and start forming it into your desired shape. Press from the edge of the base, while constantly turning the material around with your hand. Note that you are now moving a lot of material from the center to the sides of your future container, making it much larger than the original ball. You can now shape the sides of the container to your desired design and possibly smooth the container with a spoon or branch cut at the end.

THE SLAB TECHNIQUE

The slab technique — or the rolling pin technique — is a slightly more advanced method than the previous two, but the result can be really nice. With this technique, you use a rolling pin, round drinking bottle, or nicely carved, smooth piece of log.

In a similar way to making cookies, roll out the clay into ⅛ – ¼ inch (4 – 6 millimeter) thick sheets and cut them into square pieces. For example, if you want to make a mug, cut out a piece of rolled-out clay in a circle of your desired diameter. Then, take one of the rolled-out square pieces and shape it into a tube that fits the diameter of that bottom.

Make sure that the joining edge of the tube is cut diagonally so that there is as much surface as possible between the two parts for the clay to adhere to. Wet the two edges that have to adhere to each other with slip (clay dissolved in water), so they adhere well to each other. Do the same when attaching the tube to the bottom of your container, and feel free to add a thin sausage shape of clay between the tube

wall and the bottom to strengthen the container. You can now smooth the sides of the container with a spoon or cut branch.

When working with the slab technique, you run the risk of the clay sticking to the underside when rolling out. This can be remedied by first sprinkling a little flour on the surface, just like when you bake.

If you already have an existing bowl or cup, you can use it as a template for your future clay container and shape your rolled-out clay over or inside the existing bowl or cup. Be careful not to force clay down over the bowl. Let it fall naturally and gently shape it into place.

FIRING

You don't need a ceramics kiln to fire simple pottery—it can be done directly in a hot fire. Firing pottery in an open fire can be dated back to around thirty thousand years ago and was common practice until humans began to make primitive kilns where a higher temperature could be reached.

It is important that the pottery is completely dry so that it does not burst during firing. Gather your pottery on the ground and build a fire in a circle around the pottery with a good distance, 2½–3 feet (80–100 centimeters) from the pottery. Let the pottery heat up very slowly, and gradually move the fire closer and closer to the pottery over the next few hours. Make sure to maintain the fire continuously so that it has a high heat.

After six to eight hours in the middle of the fire, the pottery should be completely covered by the fire, and extra firewood can be added. The fire and the pottery should preferably end at a temperature of approximately 1,800°F (1,000°C). Now, let the fire burn out and the pottery slowly cool down, preferably until the next day.

Now, the pottery is ready for use and should not soften when it gets wet again. If you wish, you can glaze it. Note that where the pottery has not had access to oxygen during firing, it will appear charred and black. If you wish, you can provoke the black color by taking the pottery out of the fire at the end of the firing process and wrapping it in hay or straw when very hot. This process is called reduction and works in such a way that the hay is packed around the hot pottery and consumes the oxygen around the pottery, which will therefore create a black surface.

Fired pottery can be used to store food and prepare food over the fire.

WOOL FELTING

Tools: A mat or similar, soapy water.

Felted wool is the oldest textile known in human history.

Carded wool has small irregularities in the hairs, which expand when exposed to hot water, and the wool can then be massaged together in layers to your desired shape and thickness. When the wool is felted sufficiently and not exposed to more hot water, it will hold its shape and remain tangled. There are no limits to what you can felt—everything from blankets, tents, clothes, gloves, and shoes to containers has been felted over time.

It is a long process from the sheep being shorn until you have a finished felt product. First, the wool must be carded, or brushed, so that the fibers in the wool are separated. Once that is done, you can start felting with it. This is done by separating the wool into thinner layers and laying them with the fibers of the wool, crossed, possibly over a template of something like mittens or socks. The template can be made of fabric or plastic and should be made according to the measurements of the hand or foot that the finished product will fit. Now, add warm soapy water (like soap shavings that have been mixed well with water) to the wool, and massage the area of the wool that is inside the template and possibly roll it in a mat. Do not felt the edges together yet.

When the wool layers stick together well in the desired thickness, turn your

product over and add layers of wool on the other side. There should be a cavity between the two felted layers and the template should lie between the layers to prevent them from being felted together. Fold the edges around and felt them together with the other side. Remember that the felting process stops when the water gets too cold, so regularly add more warm soapy water.

When your product starts to take your desired shape (probably still in too large a size), it is time to take out the template and shape the product directly, for example, on the hand or the foot, depending on what you are making.

This is done by, again, adding warm soapy water to the product and rubbing it tightly around the hand or foot. At this stage it is still possible to move the wool around so that you get an even, thick layer all over your finished product. Be patient during this process.

When the product is finished felting, it must dry, and the edges may be cut clean of excess wool. It helps to roll and hit the wool product during felting to make the felting even tighter.

You can also felt your own wool blanket in this way; the template just needs to be a larger piece of fabric or plastic. The felting process is otherwise the same. You can also felt, for example, a bowl or bag by using an existing shape as a template. This could be a pot, a stone, or something similar.

TANNING

Tools: Scraper, possibly knife.

The processing of hides and leather is not a new invention. In fact, the tanning of hides and leather can be dated back to the Stone Age around eight thousand years before our era, when it was discovered that hides could be made waterproof and avoid decomposition by smearing them with fat from the animal itself.

Plant-based tanning was later discovered with the help of extracts from plants, like the tannic acid from oak, willow, and rubber trees.

Elsewhere in the world, the brain from the animal is used with a mixture of fat and salt to preserve the hide.

The art of tanning hides of various kinds is a whole science in itself, and there are quite a few books that go in-depth on this subject, but this book offers a few simple techniques to get you started.

In general, as it applies to tanning, the final result depends on how the hide is treated, from the moment the animal is slaughtered, until you have the finished product. This means that you have to treat the hide correctly from the very beginning to get the best result.

If you do not have the opportunity to work with the hide right after the slaughtering of the animal, it can be preserved with various methods like drying, salting, and freezing.

When drying, the hide should be stretched on a wooden frame and left in a

dry, ventilated area without constant direct sunlight. Drying removes water from the hide, which prevents microorganisms from multiplying in the hide.

Salting the hide removes water from the hide and creates a hostile environment for bacteria. Use an amount of coarse salt that corresponds to approximately 10 percent of the hide's weight to cover the flesh side of the hide. The salt absorbs fluid and blood from the skin. After a day, scrape and shake the salt off the skin and add new salt—this time, an amount corresponding to about 40 percent of the hide's weight. Make sure to cover the entire flesh side thoroughly. After another day or two, the hide can be folded together, flesh side to flesh side, and put away for storage in a cool, dry place.

Leave the salt on. The hide can be stored for approximately one year this way, but salt should be added along the way.

Freezing skin is an easy way to store it until you need it, but, of course, it requires that you have room for it in the freezer. Freezing does not stop the decomposition of the hide 100 percent, but the hide can be stored like this for about a year.

As a starting point, the hide should be softened with salting for two to four days and with drying for three to eight days, depending on which hide you work with.

The hide must now be cleaned or scraped, and here it is also important that the hide has the right consistency and isn't too wet or dry, as it will then be more difficult to scrape fat, flesh, and film from it.

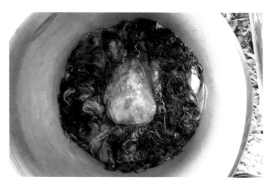

When the hide is cleaned, the actual tanning begins. It can be done in many different ways, for example, with oil/fat, salt/alum, bark/tannic acid, or chrome/chromium salt. Read more about how this is done in the following sections. The purpose of tanning is to prevent the hide from decaying and decomposing when it gets wet, as well as to retain the strength and flexibility of the hide.

When the hide is tanned, it must be softened or stretched during drying. The processes in tanning hides are therefore: any storage, cleaning, tanning, and softening. Here, I will go through some simple ways to tan different hides.

SHEEPSKIN

Sheepskin has excellent insulating properties and is naturally water-repellent due

to the high content of lanolin. This makes the hide suitable for outdoor use and as a sleeping pad or insulation in a chair.

First of all, of course, you need to get a hide. It can be obtained from a slaughterhouse or a sheep breeder and does not cost a fortune. If you don't want to tan the hide right away, it can be put in the freezer or salted well on the flesh side with ordinary coarse salt and put away until you need it.

If the hide is really dirty, it can be washed in a wool wash by hand with lukewarm water. Start the cleaning of the hide by placing it with the flesh side up on something like a tree trunk without too many irregularities. Then use ulo or, for example, steel wool with rounded corners. You can also use a scraper or a draw knife. However, none of the tools should be sharp, as this can easily damage the hide.

Now, scrape the fat, remaining flesh, tendons, and film from the hide, so that you get a nice, even surface. Start from the middle of the hide and work your way toward the edge. Keep going until the hide is nice and smooth, without fat, film, and the like. If there is still a little film left, this can be sanded off with sandpaper later.

You can now choose to wet or dry tan the hide. For wet tanning, the hide is placed in a bucket with a solution of 1 pound 6 ounces (500 grams) of alum, 1 pound 6 ounces (500 grams) of salt, and approximately 4 gallons (15 liters) of water. Make sure that the hide is completely covered by the liquid, and possibly hold it down with a stone or something similar. Leave the hide in this solution for approximately fourteen days.

If you want to dry tan the hide, you can make dough from 1 pound 6 ounces (500 grams) of alum, 1 pound 6 ounces (500 grams) each of salt, wheat flour, and water. Make sure you get thin dough that you can spread on the flesh side of your sheepskin. Then, fold it together, flesh side to flesh side, and leave it like this for approximately fourteen days.

When the tanning process is complete, rinse and hang the hide to dry. If you let the hide dry up like this, it will become completely stiff and hard. If you want a soft hide, pull the hide fibers while they dry slowly. This can be done by firmly taking hold of the hide and pulling it in all directions. The hide will become completely white and soft on the flesh side. This should be done daily throughout the drying period. You can also stretch the hide on a pole or a perpendicular edge of something like a chair until it is completely dry and soft.

If there is still some film on the hide, it can be sanded off with sandpaper to achieve a nicely finished sheepskin. This process can also be used on other hides such as deer.

FISH SKIN

A perhaps overlooked hide or leather is that from a fish. Many fish skins are incredibly strong and can be tanned and used for sacks, shopping bags, clothes, and the like. Skins from things like salmon, pike, eel, cod, and trout are well-suited for tanning and further processing.

Before you begin the tanning process of your skin, it must be cleaned of flesh, fat, and scales. Use a clam shell, putty knife, or something similar to scrape the back side clean of meat and fat residue. Use the same tool on the other side to scrape the skin free of scales. Start from the head and work your way down toward the tail to avoid damaging the scale pockets. Then, wash the skin in cool water, maximum 68°F (20°C), with a little soap, of course.

When the skin is completely clean, it should be put in a tanning liquid. Throughout time, people have used many different types of ingredients in tanning liquid, like urine, bark from oak, willow, chestnut, and brain. Oil tanning is used here, which is easy and quick to use.

For 4–5 salmon skins, you need:
- 3.4 ounces or a heaping ⅓ cup cooking oil
- 1 egg yolk
- 1 teaspoon unscented soap.

The oil and fat from the yolk soften the skin, absorb into tissue, and fill in cavities so that bacteria and decay cannot occur. Mix the aforementioned ingredients together and massage the liquid well into the skins. After 10 to 15 minutes, they are ready for the next process, which is drying and softening.

Hang the skins to dry in a warm room or out in the sun, and massage and stretch the skins continuously during the drying process. It can help to use a slightly tapered log, a chair back (as pictured), or a piece of rope tied to a tree to soften the skins during drying. This requires your full attention until the skins are completely dry. Once the skins are dry, they are difficult to soften further. The more work you put into the softening process, the nicer and softer the end product will be.

A few days after drying and softening, the skin can be further massaged with a little fat or oil to saturate it completely and soften it further. Now, you have a beautiful and very strong skin that can be used for various other projects.

BUSHCRAFT DICTIONARY

Here is a small dictionary of the most used expressions in bushcraft.

ADZE: Hollowing ax.

BANNOCK BREAD: A bread especially suitable for making over a fire. The ingredients are easy to transport, so only water needs to be added to the homemade ingredients when baking. The bread often consists of wheat flour, corn flour, sugar, dehydrated milk, and baking powder, and your choice of other added ingredients like chocolate, raisins, almonds, and other nuts.

BATON: A branch that you can use to hit the back of your knife or ax to get through the wood more easily or split it for firewood.

BOW DRILL: Used like the hand drill, but instead of using the hands, a bow is used where the cord is wrapped around the stick (spindle).

CAMPFIRE POT: A lightweight pot specially made for fires, alcohol burners, and gas burners.

CROZE: Carving tool for carving grooves with.

DUTCH OVEN: A thick-walled cast-iron pot with a tight-fitting lid that can be used for a variety of cooking over a fire. Often used with charcoal underneath, on the side, and on the lid to get an even heat all around.

FATWOOD: Coniferous wood that is filled with resin. It is usually found in roots, on the inside of branches, and where a tree is broken. When conifers, especially pine trees, break or are damaged, the trees try to heal by sending resin to the vulnerable spots, which become saturated with resin.

FIRE STEEL: It is used to make very hot sparks that can ignite kindling. Steel is considered the safest object for igniting, since it is not susceptible to moisture and can last for a long time.

FIRST AID KIT: A kit that contains the most important first aid items like patches, bandages, medicine, and a space blanket.

FLINT AND STEEL: A primitive method used to make fire. This method consists of steel with high carbon content and can be made from an old file. It can be purchased, or you can use the back of your carbon knife.

HAND DRILL: A primitive way to make fire that requires nothing more than what you can find in nature. A long branch (spindle) is rolled between the hands, where one end is pressed down against a piece of wood, and the heat that comes from the friction creates embers.

KOHLROSING: Patterns cut in wood, bone, or antler and colored with coffee grounds, ash, or something similar.

KUKSA: Cup carved from wood. Kuksa is Finnish and means "make food."

LEAN-TO SHELTER: A primitive shelter that leans against a tree, rock, or a clamped, thick branch. Often made from thick branches, leaves, and pine boughs.

PERSONAL SURVIVAL KIT: A survival kit, often in a small aluminum box. It is available in many sizes and varieties. Often includes a cutting tool and means of signaling, purifying water, procuring food, and starting a fire.

PUNKWOOD: Rotten wood.

RIDGELINE: The cord you set up between something like two trees and mount your tarp on.

SLIPKNOT: A knot that acts as a loop. With a pull on one end of the cord, the knot unties by itself.

SPACE BLANKET: A blanket made of a foil-like material that is silver-colored on one side and gold-colored on the other. The silver side can be used to reflect heat, so it reflects your body heat back or the heat from the fire toward you.

SWISS ARMY KNIFE: The well-known multi-tool with the red handle. Used by many bushcrafters worldwide.

TARP: A lightweight material that most bushcrafters use when sleeping outside, as it allows you to see nature and sleep by a fire while being protected from rain and wind.

TINDER: Kindling material.

ABOUT THE AUTHOR

Jesper Hede is one of the pioneers of bush-craft in Denmark. Since 2013, he has run the company Bushcraft Danmark, which offers classes in bushcraft, survival, and traditional old crafts.

Jesper is a well-known figure in the bush-craft community and has taught in Sweden, England, Spain, Holland, Canada, and the United States. When he is not teaching under his own auspices, he teaches at the out-door guidance program at Forest School KU (University of Copenhagen), nature schools and colleges, among other places.

THANKS TO . . .

This book would not have become a reality without the great support from the bush-craft world, countless good and nerdy con-versations around the fire, and even more hours in the forest with good people.

It would be impossible for me to thank all of those who have inspired and given me good tips over time, but I hope you know who you are . . .

SPECIAL THANKS TO

Jens Nybro for his always constructive criticism, help with the many projects, and countless fun hours together in the forest

Nikolaj Hejl for writing and helping with leather projects, and for lots of nerdy talk

John Holm for a lot of help with projects and much more

Trine Høiberg for just being fantastically lovely, for lots of fun moments, and for help with the design of the book

Jesper Weidick for inspiration and a big help with projects and great pictures

Martin Jensen for inspiration and a lot of help with projects and much more

Mette Mortensen for sparring, support, and lots of good times